This is
THAILAND

This is
THAILAND

Text by John Hoskin

Photographs by Gerald Cubitt

ASIA BOOKS

Published and distributed by
Asia Books Co., Ltd.
5 Sukhumvit Road, Soi 61,
P.O. Box 40,
Bangkok 10110, Thailand
Tel. (662) 714-0740-2 ext. 221-223
Fax. (662) 381-1621, 391-2277
e-mail: customer_serv@asiabooks.co.th

ISBN 1 85974 465 6

Commissioning Editor: Tim Jollands
Editors: Ann Baggaley, Peter Duncan
Editorial Assistant: Rowena Curtis
Designer: Alan Marshall
Cartography: Julian Baker
Index: Janet Dudley

Reproduction by HBM Print Pte, Singapore
Jacket reproduction by
Hirt and Carter, South Africa
Printed and bound in Singapore by Tien Wah
Press (Pte) Ltd

Illustrations appearing on the cover, in the preliminary pages and on the last page are as follows:

FRONT COVER: Mythological *yaksha* figures at Wat Phra Keo, Bangkok.
SPINE: The *wai*, the traditional Thai greeting.
HALF TITLE: A *poom* (flower bowl arrangement) and money trees, for donation to the temple, being carried in procession.
FRONTISPIECE: Longtail boats take visitors to the crystal-clear waters around Koh Phi Phi for superb swimming, snorkelling and diving.
TITLE PAGE: A southern Thai dancer in bejewelled helmet and beaded costume after a Manhora dance drama performance.
PAGE 5: Saffron-robed monks make their way across an ornate bridge in the compound of Bangkok's Marble Temple, Wat Benchamabophit.
PAGE 6: Intricate inlay work adorns many exteriors in Wat Phra Keo, the magnificent complex of the Temple of the Emerald Buddha.
PAGE 7: The Lotus lily is an important symbol in the Buddhist faith and a traditional motif in Thai art and culture.
PAGE 176: A topiary tree receives its daily watering at a Buddhist temple in Hua Hin, a summer retreat of the Thai Royal Family.

ACKNOWLEDGEMENTS

The author, photographer and publishers would like to express their gratitude to the following for their generous and valuable assistance during the preparation of this book:

Tourism Authority of Thailand
Think Earth/Siam Motors Co. Ltd.
Royal Forest Department, Thailand
Shangri-la Hotel, Bangkok

Sumonta Nakornthab, Terri S. Yamaka and Chalermlap Ganachara na Ayudhaya, Tourism Authority of Thailand • Phornthep Phornprapha, President, Think Earth/Siam Motors Co. Ltd. • Jeff Bacall and Fiona Pendle Harris, Bacall Harris Associates (Tourism Authority of Thailand, UK public relations) • Alan Guignon and Fiona Ferrier, Shangri-la Hotels and Resorts • Oriental Hotel, Bangkok • The Jim Thompson Foundation/Thai Silk Company Ltd, Bangkok • Khun Akorn Restaurants, London, Paris and Bangkok • Chiva Som Health Resort, Hua Hin • Royal Botanic Gardens, Kew: Dr John Dransfield, Dr Phillip Cribb, Dr Soejatmi Dransfield • Royal Botanic Garden, Edinburgh: Dr Roy Watling • Dr Charles Santiapillai • Thai Airways International • Royal Thai Embassy, London • Keith Mundy • DDFE Resources

The photographer also gratefully acknowledges the generous support of the following during his travels in Thailand:

Dusit Rayavadee Resort Hotel, Krabi • Eastern and Oriental Express, Orient Express Hotels • Imperial Tongsai Bay Hotel, Koh Samui • Le Meridien Baan Boran Hotel • Le Meridien Hotel, Phuket • Royal Cliff Beach Hotel, Pattaya • Sea Tours Co. Ltd

Ayutthaya Princess Co. Ltd • Baan Taling Ngam Resort, Koh Samui • Central Maesod Hill Hotel • Clarion M.P. Resort Hotel, Trang • Chumphon Cabana Resort • Dhevaraj Hotel, Nan • Holiday Inn, Mae Hong Son • Koh Chang Resort • Krabi Meritime Hotel • Long Beach Cha-am Hotel • Mae Nam Kong Grand View Hotel, Nakhon Phanom • Melia Hotel, Hua Hin • Pailyn Hotel, Phitsanulok • Phang-Nga Bay Resort Hotel • Phi Phi Palm Beach Hotel • Pimarn Hotel, Nakhon Sawan • River View Lodge, Chiang Mai • Royal Crown Hotel, Songkhla • Royal Princess Hotel, Khorat • Tanyong Hotel, Narathiwat • Wang Tai Hotel, Surat Thani

Special Photographer's Acknowledgement
The photographer wishes to express his great debt of gratitude to his wife, Janet, who accompanied him throughout his travels in Thailand, providing not only practical support but also insight and perception into every aspect of the photography.

CONTENTS

PREFACE

Just as a master chef combines secret ingredients and flair to create wonderful dishes, Thailand blends beauty, charm and character to provide visitors with a never-ending spectrum of pleasures that delight the senses, yet still leave them hungry for more.

This perhaps explains why so many tourists return year after year to continue exploring our almost limitless list of attractions, enjoy the wide range of sports, or take in a round of golf on one of our 150 fine courses. Others come back to learn our rich language, trek in the national parks, study our proud history and culture, master our famous cuisine, research our herbal medicine and ancient techniques of massage, or retreat to one of the many temples to meditate and acquire the timeless wisdom of the Lord Buddha.

The words 'Amazing' and 'Enchantment' have been used to describe Thailand with good reason, for beyond the superb sightseeing and shopping lies an elusive magic, which is difficult to define.

Does it lie in the wonderful costumes and customs of hilltribes in the misty North? In the idyllic settings of the Golden Triangle and the mighty Mekong? In the warm hospitality of Isarn? In the dynamic energy of Bangkok? On the sun-soaked beaches and islands of the South? In the ancient stones of our historical monuments? In the clamour and colour of our bustling markets? In the aesthetic beauty of the Grand Palace? Or in the spontaneous smiles which greet you from any school playground? Or in all of the above?

Whether you are a first time visitor, or an old hand, this informative and well-written book will guide you beautifully through what there is to do, see, experience and most likely, still leave you longing for more. One thing is for sure; no matter how much you experience Amazing Thailand, you will never have enough.

This, indeed, is Thailand.

Pradech Phayakvichien
Governor
Tourism Authority of Thailand

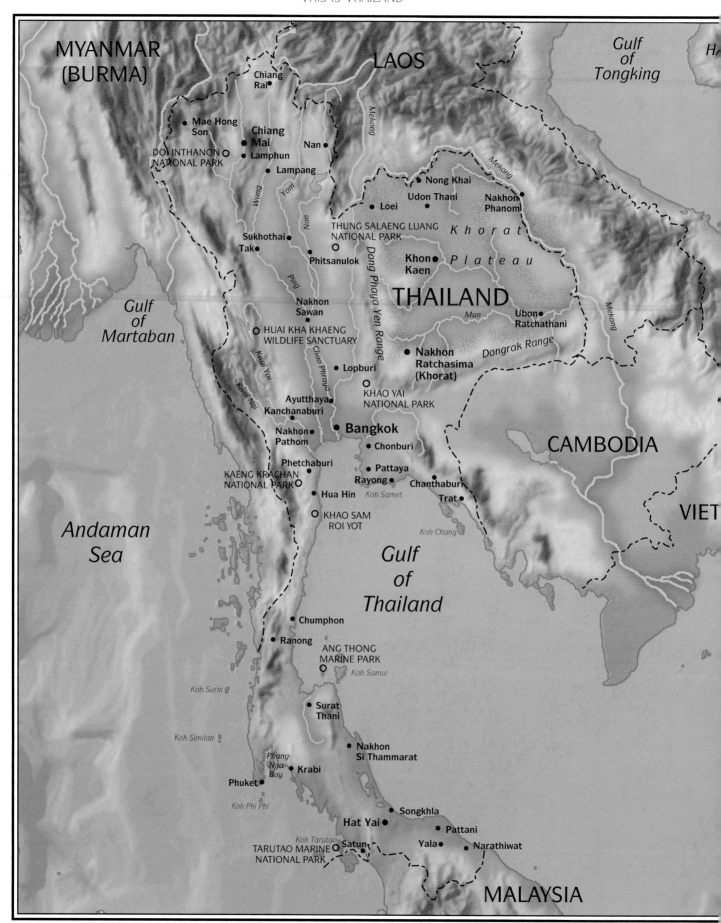

N

THAILAND

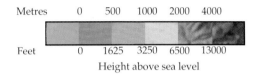

| 0 | 250 | 500 | 750 | 1000 km |

| 0 | 125 | 250 | 375 | 500 | 625 miles |

| Metres | 0 | 500 | 1000 | 2000 | 4000 |

| Feet | 0 | 1625 | 3250 | 6500 | 13000 |

Height above sea level

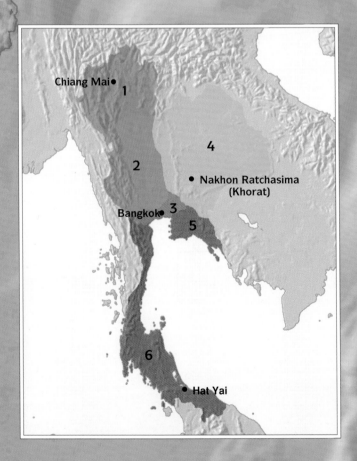

JOURNEY THROUGH THAILAND

The areas covered by the chapters
in **Journey through Thailand** are ordered
according to the following sequence.

PROFILE OF THAILAND

An elevated tollway leads from the airport into Bangkok, a stream of vehicles passing over an even greater flow of cars, buses and trucks on the highway beneath. The cityscape bristles with high-rise offices, condominiums, luxury hotels and shopping plazas, while weaving its way between is the raised track of the Skytrain, Bangkok's first mass transit system opened in December 1999. Then, as the taxi passes one of the busiest downtown intersections, the scene of urban chaos is fleetingly replaced by a glimpse of classical oriental wonder. There, on the street corner, is an ornate little shrine housing a gilded statue of the four-headed, eight-armed god Brahma. Devotees clutching smouldering sticks of incense make offerings, while elaborately costumed classical dancers weave slow, sinuous movements in an atmosphere heady with the scent of jasmine. It is a daily scene at the Erawan Shrine, which, regardless of the surrounding modern world, is still believed to be Thailand's most potent source of good fortune.

All countries are different but some are more different than others, and Thailand is happily and uniquely itself. Throughout 700 years of independence, the Thai Kingdom has displayed an amazing continuity, underpinned by the people's unwavering adherence to Buddhism, the national religion, and to the monarchy.

Thailand conjures in most minds striking images of golden spires and sweeping temple roofs, of emerald paddy fields, forested hills and elephants, of travel poster clichés depicting white sandy beaches fringed by palms. Such scenes are to be found, but popular conceptions give only part of the picture, and the land, its people and their history make up a complex nation with its own distinct characteristics.

As the 20th century draws to a close, Thailand is undergoing unprecedented growth and change as increasing prosperity, Westernization and a growing society of young urban professionals challenge the old ways without posing any clear alternatives. Cause for concern perhaps, but the most remarkable characteristic of the Thais has always been their resilience. It is all a balancing act, and the underlying quality of Thai-ness maintains the quintessential paradox of Thailand's Janus stance as it looks to the past with pride and to the future with confidence.

THE LAND

What is an extraordinarily rich and diverse land arises from Thailand's geographical make up. Located within the latitudes 6 degrees and 21 degrees north, Thailand extends 1,650 kilometres (1,025 miles) north to south and 800 kilometres (500 miles) east to west. The shape of the country is extremely irregular – often fancifully likened to an elephant's head, with its trunk extending down to the Malay Peninsula — and produces a topographical range running from forested mountains and steep river valleys in the north to a long narrow southern peninsula with a coastline touched by both the Indian Ocean and the inshore extensions of the Pacific Ocean, and fringed with tropical beaches and offshore islands. Between these extremes lie the rich agricultural lands of central Thailand, while to the east is the semi-arid Khorat Plateau.

Situated in the heart of South-east Asia, the country occupies 513,115 square kilometres (198,114 square miles), an area roughly the size of France, and is bordered by Myanmar (Burma) in the west, Laos in the north-east, Cambodia in the east and Malaysia in the south. The landmass lies between two mountain systems – the Central Cordillera in the west and the Cordillera of Annam in the east – and divides into six topographical regions: the North, the Central Plains, the North-east, the South-east, the West and the Southern peninsula.

Northern Thailand, covering about one-quarter of the nation's area, is primarily a region of parallel mountain ranges running north to south and divided by steep, fertile river valleys. Most of the hills are between 500 and 1,000 metres (1,600–3,000 feet) in elevation, although five peaks rise over 2,000 metres (6,500 feet). Doi Inthanon, south of Chiang Mai, is the kingdom's highest mountain at 2,565 metres (8,415 feet). The lower hills are typically covered with deciduous forests, where teak was once dominant. However, excessive logging, combined with the slash-and-burn agriculture of the hilltribe people who have long inhabited the upland areas, has resulted in the serious depletion of forest cover. Above 1,000 metres (3,000 feet), the mountains support evergreen forests harbouring a wealth of plant and animal species.

The area forms a vital watershed region and in the mountains are the headwaters of four principal rivers, the Ping, Wang, Yom and Nan, which flow south to join the Chao Phraya river, Thailand's major waterway. Although most of the water run-off is to the south, the basins of the far north flow north-east to feed the Mekong river.

Directly below the northern region and extending 450 kilometres (290 miles) down to the Gulf of Thailand are the Central Plains, the nation's heartland. This characteristically flat region is dominated by the Chao Phraya river, which supports an extensive and highly developed network of canals and irrigation projects to form the kingdom's 'rice bowl'. Made intensely fertile by rich alluvial deposits, the countryside presents archetypal images of an exotic Asian land, typified by a patchwork of paddy fields, broken here and there by stands of palms between which glint the gilded spires and soaring roofs of village temples. The concentrated rural population of the Central Plains is startlingly contrasted at the region's south-eastern edge, at the head of the Gulf, where Bangkok, the hub of the nation's industrial and commercial activity, sprawls like an urban pancake.

A further marked contrast is found in the North-east, where the extensive Khorat Plateau rises some 300 metres (1,000 feet) above the Central Plains. The area covers about one-third of the country and is bounded in the south by the Dongrak mountains, which form the border with Cambodia, and on the west by the flat-topped Dong Phaya Yen mountains. Ringed by the Mekong river in the north and east, the region is essentially a large basin, drained by the Mun and other smaller tributaries of the Mekong.

Known as *I-san* in Thai, the North-east is the poorest and least developed part of the country, its economy scarcely rising above subsistence farming. A once dense cover of deciduous forest has been almost totally destroyed by man's encroachment, and much of the land is poor, subject to seasonal droughts and floods, while the soil is often salty. The landscape is not all bleak, however. Pockets of forest cover have survived due, ironically, to political insecurity in parts of the North-east, where strongholds of communist insurgency existed in the 1970s and where, in the 1980s and 1990s, Cambodian resistance forces have operated in the southern border areas.

Unlike I-san, the South-east has undergone dramatic change over the last two decades. The smallest of Thailand's topographical regions, forming a wedge of land between the Gulf of Thailand and the mountains of south-west Cambodia, the area comprises a narrow coastal plain backed by a hinterland of low hills. Traditionally, much of the land has been commercially produc-

Above: *Typical of northern Thailand's landscape are fertile valleys and forested mountains, here encircling Mae Hong Son.*

PREVIOUS PAGES
Page 10: *Elaborately costumed performers execute the graceful movements of the classical* lakon nai *dance drama.*
Page 11: *Thai children hold their hands in the* wai, *the traditional Thai greeting.*

Rice fields cover much of Thailand's rural landscape in the North as well as in the Central Plains, the nation's rice bowl.

Off Thailand's southern peninsula lie numerous tropical islands, many, such as Koh Samui, edged with palm-fringed, white-sand beaches.

tive, both in fresh produce, notably fruits and spices, and in sapphires and rubies mined in the south-easternmost provinces of Chanthaburi and Trat.

Today a new prosperity is taking over the area and what is now called the Eastern Seaboard has, since the mid-1980s, been extensively developed as an industrial and tourism zone, while the hinterland has been transformed by the construction of new highways giving access to Bangkok and to the North-east. Much of the indented coastline is dotted with rocky offshore islands. Many of these are still forested, although some, like Koh Chang, are now being groomed as tourist resorts.

The West of Thailand, straddling the area between Bangkok and the Burmese border, forms a continuation of the northern mountains, although the valleys are smaller and the plains fewer. Several tributaries of the Chao Phraya and Salween rivers rise in the mountains, while the main river system is that of the Kwai Yai and Kwai Noi which join to form the Mae Khlong at Kanchanaburi, site of the infamous Bridge over the River Kwai built by allied POWs during World War II. In spite of tourism development in the valleys of the Kwai Yai and Kwai Noi, the West contains some of Thailand's richest surviving forest covers.

The last topographical region, the Southern peninsula, is a long sliver of land with a steep mountainous spine, a continuation of the western uplands and rising to more than 1,800 metres (5,900 feet). Extending from central Thailand down to the Malaysian border, the area is characterized by sheer humped formations of limestone karst, which appear as both inland cliffs and offshore islets. The climate and habitat are close to those of the true rainforest, and the flora and fauna are similar to those of Malaysia rather than the predominantly Indo-Burmese varieties of the continental lowlands. Rubber and coconut cultivation, as well as tin mining, are the traditional economic activities of the region.

The western coast of the peninsula, bordered by the Andaman Sea, is very irregular and indented with estuaries and mangrove inlets. It is also strung with offshore islands, including Thailand's largest island, Phuket, connected to the mainland by a causeway. On the eastern shore, facing the Gulf of Thailand, are long stretches of beach.

THE SEASONAL CYCLE

It has been a sunny June morning when, suddenly, in mid-afternoon dark clouds have gathered seemingly out of nowhere and with no more warning the heavens

open. Just a half-hour downpour during the rainy season and modern Bangkok transforms itself to mock its old soubriquet, 'Venice of the East', except it is no longer canals but flooded streets that criss-cross the city.

Low-lying on an alluvial plain, Bangkok is especially susceptible to flooding when the monsoon rains coincide with a high tide on the Chao Phraya river. Even modest rainfall can produce depressingly familiar scenes of watery weariness – office girls clutching their shoes and wading knee deep; shopkeepers piling sandbags across their doorways; residents paddling sampans down side streets. Generally it is all accepted with good grace, and so it should be as Thailand has traditionally depended on, and prospered from, the annual rains.

An idea of just how vital the rains are is vividly illustrated by scenes of the semi-arid North-east during the hottest months of April and May. Earth, baked rock hard by the relentless sun, cracks and deep fissures pattern the land like fractured safety glass.

But too much or too little rain is relative, and while Thailand can be mildly uncomfortable for brief moments of the year, the country is in the main extremely fortunate when compared to the drought-ridden or flood-devastated lands of other parts of

During the rainy season, when the Buddhist Rains Retreat is celebrated, vivid green rice plants shoot up to form an emerald patchwork of paddy fields.

Asia. It is totally free of virtually all the natural catastrophes suffered by its neighbours, the volcanic eruptions and perennial typhoons which wreak havoc in, for example, the Philippines.

The rhythm of the year is set by Thailand's tropical climate, which is dominated by alternating monsoons producing three seasons, although the climatic shifts are not necessarily appreciable to temperate-clime visitors, who tend to find the country hot and humid whatever the month. From the farmer's point of view, however,

The Songkran Festival celebrates the Thai New Year; passers-by are splashed, and often soaked, with water.

these timely monsoonal changes are vital.

The south-west monsoon prevails from around June to mid-October and carries moisture from the Indian Ocean, producing the wet season which accounts for most of the country's average annual rainfall of 1,550 millimetres (60 inches). From mid-October to mid-February the wind shifts with the north-east monsoon bringing dry air from China and producing a so-called cool season. The third, hot, season comes in the months of March, April and May. The average annual temperature range is from 30°C (100°F) to 19°C (66°F).

The traditional Thai year dawns in the hottest month of April, New Year's Day falling on 13 April and marked by the Songkran Festival, when water is sprinkled over Buddha images as ritual of cleansing, and splashed over one and all in a less than spiritual mark of the festivities. But the seasonal cycle dictating the agricultural year more properly begins with the advent of the rains in late May or June.

Throughout, the cycle is punctuated by time-honoured ceremonies and festivals, which serve both as holidays from the toil of agricultural work and as rituals serving the ancient beliefs that underpin village life. Some occasions, such as the Ploughing Ceremony, are national affairs; others, such as the Rocket Festival in the North-east,

held in May to ensure plentiful rains, are peculiar to specific regions.

As the earth softens with the early downpours, the soil, previously baked hard during the inactive hot season, yields to the plough, turning thick and moist. Mechanization has yet to alter the timeless scene, and although a few farmers may now use a small mechanical plough, the vast majority continue to rely on the strength of water buffalo. Once the fields have been prepared, the arduous task of transplanting rice seedlings begins. Working in lines, backs bent and heads covered with scarves and straw hats, men, women and children laboriously root the young plants in the flooded earth. Gradually the countryside assumes a brilliant hue as vivid green rice shoots carpet the land.

While the new crop slowly matures, the annual three-month Buddhist Rains Retreat is celebrated. It is a time when Buddhist monks remain in their monasteries, although the tradition predates Buddhism and is derived from ancient India, where itinerant holy men would pass the rainy season in permanent dwelling, lest in their wanderings they might inadvertently tread on freshly planted crops.

By the end of October, with the rains drawing to a close, the air cools and the paddy fields turn golden yellow as the rice ripens. The night of the full moon in November, before harvest time, is the occasion for the most enchanting of the festivals that punctuate the Thai year, Loy Krathong. The word loy means 'to float' and a krathong is a little lotus-shaped vessel made of banana leaves and containing flowers, incense sticks, a candle and a coin as offering to Mae Khongkha, goddess of rivers and waterways. By moonlight, people throughout the country, in Bangkok as well as in the tiniest village, gather on the banks of rivers, lakes and ponds to float their krathongs so that they may carry away the past year's sins, as well as send forth wishes for good fortune in the future.

In late November or early December, the rice crop is fully ripe and the year end is a busy time for the entire rural community, with everyone, young and old, toiling long hours to gather in the harvest. With the crop gathered and the stubble burnt off, an air of quiet tropical ease descends over village life, and the non-productive hot months provide time to make repairs around the farm and tend secondary crops.

AN AQUATIC LIFE

Throughout South-east Asia, rivers have played a crucial role in the rise of civilizations. With wet rice cultivation as the people's staple support, populations grew up in the valleys, basins and delta areas of the region's major waterways. Water made the lands fertile and provided ready transportation links. Basically, whoever held the river valleys and flood plains ruled.

This pattern is especially clear in Thailand, where nearly all settlements, from capital cities to villages, were essentially aquatic, founded on the banks of rivers whose natural waters were vastly extended by networks of canals. The former capital of Ayutthaya, at its height in the 17th century, had more than 140 kilometres (85 miles) of canals. The most important of the rivers, the Chao Phraya – 'River of Kings'– flows a mere 365 kilometres (227 miles) through the Central Plains and out into the Gulf of Thailand. Yet its modest length is misleading and the Chao Phraya has played a crucial role in the country's historical development, being not only the life source of the fertile heartland, but also a vital communications artery and strategic location for past and present capitals.

Even today, the river remains a significant highway. Many people commute daily to central Bangkok from Thonburi on the west bank and from the northern suburb of Nonthaburi. Serving this traffic are Chao Phraya express ferry boats that criss-cross the river, picking up and dropping off passengers at the score or so landing stages on both banks. Other smaller craft ply a simple back-and-forth ferry service at various points, while travellers in a hurry can hire a longtail boat, a sleek craft powered by a huge outboard engine that speeds across the water sending out a wake that rocks more somnolent riverusers. Ferries and longtail boats do not have the river to themselves. The Chao Phraya retains something of its old importance as a major highway linking Bangkok with the upcountry provinces and continues to serve longhaul transportation.

With waterways serving as transport links, the river and its attendant canals also served as market places. As every tourist today knows, the so-called 'Floating Market' on the outskirts of Bangkok is a priority sight even now, and if it has become over-commercialized by the tourist industry, the traveller does not have to journey far upstream to glimpse authentic scenes of traditional riverine lifestyles that have scarcely changed over the years – little wooden houses, built high on stilts, fronting the water's edge, youngsters splashing about, girls bathing demurely in their sarongs, men fishing lazily from sampans.

Complementing the inland waterways are some 2,500 kilometres (1,550 miles) of coastline, and while the Thais have never been great seafarers, they have been inveterate fishermen. Until manufacturing overtook traditional economic activities in the 1980s, fishing ranked second to agriculture in both extent and value among Thailand's basic industries. In recent years, while commercial fishing has remained important, over-fishing and destructive practices such as dynamiting have had an adverse effect on fish stocks in both the Gulf of Thailand and the coastal waters of the Andaman Sea.

In an attempt to offset declining marine stocks, the government has encouraged the development of fish and shrimp farms, although this has led to the destruction or degrading of mangrove forests, one of the most biologically productive habitats. However, old-style fishing villages have not entirely vanished. The sight of fish drying in the sun on racks of split bamboo is still common, and the elaborately painted *kawlae* boats traditional to the largely Muslim fishing communities of the southernmost provinces still add a rainbow of colours against the white sand of the beaches.

FORESTS

Travellers driving from the northern Thai capital of Chiang Mai to the nearby historic town of Lamphun cannot help but marvel at the huge, 30-metre-tall (100-foot) trees flanking the old road. Miraculously preserved and meticulously pruned, they stand in marked contrast to the ever-spreading suburbs of the city.

A thin row though they are today, these trees are remarkable in giving a vivid impression of the forests that once covered virtually the entire country. Even up until about 60 years ago some 70 per cent of Thailand's land area was forested, but human encroachment and excessive commercial logging have taken their toll in recent decades, and official estimates now put forest cover at 25-28 per cent, although most independent observers believe the true figure to be much lower.

Rivers and canals continue to play a useful part in the transportation of goods and people; a number of waterways still serve as floating marketplaces.

Unlike in temperate climates, where forests comprise generally a single type of tree, Thailand displays an immense variety of forest. Evergreen rainforests are found in the Southern peninsula and other areas with high rainfall, and are dominated by trees of the dipterocarp family, some of which form a topmost canopy rising to a height of 50 metres (165 feet). Beneath the canopy are several layers of bamboos and palms, with herbs and small shrubs at the lowest level on the forest floor. In the upland areas of continental Thailand, the similar but drier semi-evergreen forest is usually found, a considerable proportion of it protected by conservation areas. Drier lowland areas support the seasonal mixed deciduous and deciduous dipterocarp forests, which are lighter and airier than the rainforests and also very beautiful when their leaves change colour before falling. Different again are the pine forests which grow in areas of sandy soil in parts of the North and North-east. Mangrove forests were once widespread in the coastal areas, but most are now either destroyed or degraded. Within these broad divisions of forest types are several subcategories, as well as considerable intermingling of evergreen and deciduous.

The variety of Thailand's forests is enhanced by a richness of flowering trees and plants, with over 1,000 species of orchids as well as a huge variety of ferns, creepers and vines. In areas where forests have been preserved, such a wealth of flora offers the possibility of near endless botanical discovery within even just a small area.

THE WILDLIFE

MAMMALS

Counted among Thailand's nearly 300 types of mammals are Asian Elephants, deer, Gaur (the Asian Bison), bears, the Tiger, the rare Clouded Leopard and several species of the smaller wild cats, monkeys and gibbons. Besides other interesting small mammals, such as wild dogs, otters, civets and mongooses, Thailand can boast over 100 bat species. These range from the large Flying Fox to the so-called 'bumble-bee' bat, which is the world's smallest mammal and now very rare. In areas where there are caves, huge colonies of the commoner bats

will gather to roost, streaming out of the cave mouths in the deepening dusk.

Sadly the numbers of nearly all Thailand's large animals are in serious decline. Man has generally been the culprit. Not only have animal populations been reduced by hunting, the capture of certain wild animals has long held a fascination. Even today, gibbons are still sold as pets, although conservationists are beginning to make headway in the struggle against trade in wild animals and, worse, animal parts which are valued especially by the Chinese for their supposed medicinal properties.

Perhaps the worst affected of Thailand's

Most of Thailand's exquisite orchids, such as this Dendrobium *species, are epiphytic, growing high up in forest trees.*

large animals is the Tiger. Up until about 50 years ago, travellers commonly remarked on how parts of the country were infested with these creatures, and it seemed almost obligatory to recount at least one close call. Now the Tiger is vanishing from Thailand at an alarming rate, the current population being estimated at only about 250, the animals doing little better than clinging to survival in tiny 'islands' of habitat.

Facing equally uncertain prospects is the Asian Elephant. That it also is declining in numbers is to be doubly regretted as the elephant, more than any other creature, is emblematic of the country.

In ancient times, war elephants were effective fighting machines, the forerunner of the tank and the mount of kings and princes who would enter into one-to-one combat on the back of a specially trained beast. The white or albino elephant has also long been held in high esteem, and all such creatures continue to be the sole property of the King, the possession of one or more presaging well for the success of the reign.

The elephant is also the stuff of legends and is featured in numerous classical tales and religious myths, but it is as a work animal that it has contributed most, serving in the past as both a pack animal and as a labourer in the teak forests. Amazingly sure-footed, it can be trained in various skills to lift, push, stack and haul heavy objects. Making it superior to machines in forestry work is the elephant's ability to manoeuvre logs in rugged terrain without the necessity of constructing roads that would harm the environment.

The logging ban of 1989 has now made the work elephant virtually redundant. Some young elephant training schools remain in the North, primarily as showcases where tourists can see the animals' skills, but the sad fact is that both domesticated and wild elephants are in decline. At the turn of the century there were more than 100,000 domesticated elephants in Thailand; today there are around 5,000. Wild elephants are believed to number between 2,000 to 3,000, in both protected and non-protected areas. The decline is due primarily to habitat loss and to poaching of ivory and meat.

Even without a declining population, elephants are notoriously difficult to see as, in spite of their immense size, the animals are shy and secretive. The largest wild population in a protected area, with numbers estimated at 200, is found at Khao Yai National Park, near Bangkok.

In the last 35 years over 100 conservation areas have been established in Thailand, covering a wide variety of habitats and protecting a rich diversity of animal species. Some of these are open to the public, combining conservation and tourism.

BIRDS

Because of its location at a 'zoogeographic crossroads', Thailand boasts one of the richest bird faunas in Asia. The majority of Thailand's birds are found in national parks and other sanctuaries, and it is the forested areas which have the most to offer the bird-watcher. Perhaps the finest of all is the Great Hornbill, the largest of 12 species of hornbills found in the country. With a huge black and white body, broad barred tail, golden-yellow neck, black mask and thick curving beak surmounted by a horny casque, it makes an impressive sight in flight, though it is ungainly out of its natural element and its arrival at a tree seems more like a crash landing than a graceful descent. Hornbills are social and noisy birds with such a raucous honk that a pair in duet can sound startlingly like some prehistoric beast to anyone standing nearby.

As retiring as the hornbills are intrusive are the pittas of which there are 12 species in Thailand, the most widespread being the Blue Pitta. These pretty forest birds are shy and largely terrestrial in habit, which makes them notoriously inconspicuous. Many other species are more easily observed, however, and these include the brightly coloured trogons, kingfishers and a variety of bulbuls, leafbirds and drongos.

Constituting a huge family of resident Oriental birds are the vocal and gregarious babblers – jungle babblers, scimitar-babblers, laughingthrushes, minlas and fulvettas. The greatest variety inhabits the northern mountains, although representatives can be seen in virtually all forest areas. Numbered among Thailand's wealth of other small birds are warblers, thrushes, flycatchers, sunbirds and flowerpeckers.

The narrow Southern peninsula is a major route for migratory hawks heading south to Malaysia and Sumatra. Although these birds are often spiralling on thermal updrafts to heights of approximately 300 metres (1,000 feet) or more and so not easy to observe, clouds and rain squalls may force them to fly lower, offering a wonderful sight. Among the numerous predatory species seen in Thailand are the Black Baza, Crested Honey-buzzard, Japanese Sparrowhawk, Chinese Goshawk and Grey-faced Buzzard.

An impressive array of large waterbirds was also once resident in Thailand, among them the Spot-billed Pelican, Sarus Crane, Black-necked Stork and Ibis. This is sadly

Thailand's largest mammal, the elephant, has always played an important role in Thai life and culture. As a working animal in the teak forest its days are over but its skills and might can still be witnessed in northern training camps.

no longer the case due to vanishing habitats, though on the positive side, the Asian Openbill Stork is still present in significant numbers, while cormorants, egrets and night-herons remain fairly numerous.

Adding considerably to the country's resident bird populations are some 240 species of both waterbirds and landbirds which visit during the winter. Best known though not necessarily best liked by Bangkok residents are the barn swallows which congregate at night in huge numbers on trees, building ledges and overhead cables in the heart of the capital. In fact, birdwatchers need not venture further than Bangkok to get an inkling of the nation's wealth of avifauna. Beside the barn swallows, more than 150 species of birds have been sighted in and around the capital, including cuckoos, bulbuls, Oriental magpie-robins, tailorbirds, pied fantails, flowerpeckers and four species of mynas.

Thailand's fauna is among the richest in South-east Asia. Rarely seen, and now clinging to survival in protected forests, is the majestic Tiger (below left). Other forest dwellers include the black-bibbed Pileated Gibbon (left), the beady-eyed Wreathed Hornbill (below right) – both owners of distinctive forest calls – and the silent but venomous Green Pit Viper (opposite, below left). Thailand's national bird is the Siamese Fireback Pheasant (far left).

MARINE LIFE

The diversity of wildlife on the land is paralleled by the rich marine world of Thailand's coastline and surrounding seas. Just as the country's long north-south extent provides different habitats, so do the western and eastern shores offer varied marine worlds. The Andaman Sea, on the west, includes flora and fauna characteristic of the Indian Ocean, while the Gulf of Thailand, on the eastern side, is influenced by the Indo-Pacific region.

Dotted with numerous offshore islands, the coastline of the Andaman Sea is one of stunning beauty. Round Phuket Island, internationally renowned as one of the world's most beautiful tropical resorts, coral reefs –the underwater equivalent of the rainforest as one of nature's richest habitats – harbour more than 400 species of fish and in excess of 250 species of hard corals. The realm they present is truly fantastic and has gained a high reputation with divers.

In addition to commercially valuable fish, there are also game fish such as marlin, sailfish, barracudas and a variety of sharks, typically tigers and makos. Other less numerous but exotic inhabitants include manta rays and giant marine turtles. Also once common was the Dugong or 'sea cow', a marine mammal which feeds on sea grass, but this seal-like creature is now extremely rare having suffered from centuries of hunting, and the Fisheries Department has declared it a protected species.

Shallower and not as clear as the Andaman Sea, the waters of the Gulf of Thailand are more sheltered from oceanic elements. They are less productive in corals although rich in open-water fish such as mackerel, sardine and anchovies.

Like the terrestrial environment, the marine world has suffered at the hands of man. Virtually all habitats – coral reef, mangrove swamp and pelagic (open water) – are under threat from a variety of sources, including pollution in various forms and largely unregulated tourism development.

REPTILES AND AMPHIBIANS

Snakes top many people's list of creatures to be feared and Thailand numbers at least 176 species, of which about one-third are extremely poisonous, a third mildly so and the remainder non-venomous. In reality, the number of fatal snake bites recorded each year is extremely low.

The snake with the most fearsome reputation is the King Cobra, which can grow to a length of more than 5 metres (16 feet) and have a girth as big as a muscular man's forearm. Its size and volume of venom delivered make it the most dangerous of Thailand's serpents, and elephants and water buffalo have been known to succumb to bites. King Cobras are fairly widespread in forests and plantations. Thailand's other cobras are the common Monocled Cobra, found throughout the country, and the Spitting Cobra, which is capable of spitting venom over a distance of a couple of metres with considerable accuracy, and favours well-drained upland areas.

The flora of the Kingdom is as diverse as its fauna. With a rich variety of habitats in which to flourish, the flowering plants of Thailand range from the rhododendrons (right) of its northern mountains to the Lotus lilies (below right) of its lagoons and lakes. Off its tropical coasts lie the wonders of the underwater realm: a spectacular profusion of coral reefs (far right) and teeming marine life, including turtles, rays and even an occasional elusive Dugong.

For size there is nothing to beat the python, with the Reticulated Python growing up to 10 metres (30 feet) or more. The other two species found in Thailand, the Blood Python and the Rock Python, are considerably smaller. Beautifully marked, they are handsome and immensely powerful snakes, that can strike with speed, suffocating their prey by constriction.

Of other snakes, and often the most startlingly beautiful, there are 14 species of vipers, 10 of which inhabit trees and can be glimpsed gliding through the branches in search of small lizards. Deadliest are the Russell's Viper and the Malayan Pit Viper, which account for the larger number of venomous snake bites.

Once as feared as snakes, the crocodile has fared less well in Thailand. Both the freshwater and the saltwater species are now all but locally extinct, having suffered from the hunter and from loss of habitat. Some may still exist in remote areas, but the only realistic chance of spotting the beast is at one of the crocodile farms near Bangkok, where the animals are reared for their skins, serving as tourist attractions before ending up as handbags and shoes.

Three species of the terrestrial tortoise make their home in Thailand, and are found in most areas except the marshy central plains. Freshwater turtles outside of temple ponds and pools are now rare and virtually all the 18 or so species found in Thailand are endangered. Giant marine turtles come to lay their eggs on the beaches of Thailand's southern shores during September to February. The largest of all is the Leatherback, weighing up to 900 kilograms (2,000 pounds). Ridley's Turtles and a few Green Turtles and Hawksbills are also visitors to the southernmost shores.

Completing the reptilian and amphibian world are numerous species of frogs and toads, their croaks loudly punctuating the night air during the rainy season, and a great variety of lizards, ranging from the more than 2-metre (6-foot) long monitors to tiny skinks. So common as to be almost characteristic of the Thai home are the geckos. Not only useful in feeding on insects, the Common House Gecko, or *jingjok*, is an entertaining little creature, defying gravity with its adhesive toe pads which allow it to scuttle up smooth surfaces and across ceilings with ease.

Also familiar is the gecko known as a tokay, so named for the sound of its distinctive deep-throated call. Fat and with its greyish skin mottled with blue and orange spots, it not as friendly-looking as the *jingjok*, but the Thais believe it is a lucky omen if its call is heard repeated nine times. It never is and the tokay rarely calls more than five times in succession.

INSECTS

Nowhere is Thailand's rich natural diversity more apparent than in its insect life. Perhaps not the most obviously attractive of nature's realms – popularly considered as little more than a source of pests and irritating bites – the insect world is full of amazement and beauty that often goes unappreciated. Tropic nights, for example, would not be the same without the shrill rasping of the cicadas and the hypnotic sound of countless other insects.

No one can hazard a guess at precisely how many species of insects are found in Thailand, all that is certain is that many remain to be discovered. What is known, however, is staggering enough and, for example, there are an estimated 10,000 species of beetles, some 1,200 butterflies and close to 200 species of hawk moths. Thailand's butterflies outshine even birds in the beauty and brilliance of their colours, and on a stroll in a forest park many different species can be seen, fluttering gently in the air or clustered around some flowering shrub. As exotic as their looks are their names — windmills, swordtails, dragontails, courtesans, marquis and a host more.

THE HISTORY OF THAILAND

HISTORICAL INDEPENDENCE
Throughout its historical development Thailand, or Siam as it was known until well into the 20th century, has displayed marked continuity, compared to its neighbours, and is unique in the history of South-east Asia in that it was never colonized by a Western power – a fact in which the Thais take enormous pride. Although there was considerable European intervention during the development of the modern state, and Western models were followed in shaping political, social and economic institutions, Thailand is distinguished by certain historical traits and characteristics that have remained constant.

Primarily, the Thais have been rice cultivators and devout Buddhists, content to leave government in the hands of an educated élite. The social order has been hierarchical, based on wealth, status and influence; maintaining the equilibrium was an acceptance of the obligations of status and the reciprocation of services rendered.

The nation's cultural, social and political roots can be traced back centuries to the early Thai kingdoms, and the idea of the past – in which myth and legend are mixed with historical fact – has served to sustain national identity in spite of borrowings from regional predecessors as well as from the West. This identity has three symbolic foundations in the monarchy, Buddhism and nationhood, the first two in particular being quintessential to an understanding of Thailand's history.

PREHISTORY
Located on the migrationary route from southern China, Thailand has attracted

Excavations at Ban Chiang revealed a wealth of painted pottery, evidence of a flourishing prehistoric culture.

diverse peoples since prehistoric times. Ample archaeological evidence suggests the existence of a thriving Paleolithic culture in the region, which has probably supported continuous human habitation for at least 20,000 years.

Thailand's original inhabitants were likely to have been non-Mongoloid peoples, perhaps Negritos or Polynesians. While little is known about these earliest settlers, excavations conducted in the 1970s at Ban Chiang in north-eastern Thailand indicate an advanced culture flourishing in the area as far back as 3600 BC.

It would appear that the land was first populated by diverse waves of immigration, attracted to the area by the fertility of the land, most especially the Chao Phraya river basin. By the end of the first millennium BC, tribal territories in peninsular South-east Asia had begun to coalesce into protohistorical kingdoms, the earliest of which was Funan, centred on the Mekong Delta, now part of Vietnam. Ultimately, through a steady and prolonged migration, the Thais entered the region from their original homeland in southern China, and eventually rose to become the dominant force in the peninsula. Prior to their ascendancy, however, various influences were at work, establishing a pattern of civilization to which the Thais became cultural heirs.

EARLY KINGDOMS
Fundamental to the cultural development of the entire Indochina peninsula was the impact of ancient India. Social, religious and artistic roots can all be traced back to this shaping force. In the first centuries AD Indian traders were crossing the Bay of Bengal and venturing into the Far East. Because of the types of ships they sailed and the prevailing seasonal monsoons, their journeys east and south required stops at ports along the Indochina peninsula. During these sojourns a process of Indianization very gradually took place. The merchants themselves probably had little lasting impact on the indigenous cultures and it was more likely that Indian princes set themselves up to rule over petty states, marrying into the local population to legitimize their authority.

The process of Indianization formed a cultural base out of which developed a number of independent kingdoms in the centuries before the rise of the Thai. Three, in particular, were especially formative on what would later become Thailand.

The first of these, Dvaravati, was a vaguely united group of Mon people, who had entered the region probably from southern China and settled in a collection of city states with, most likely, a power base at what is now Nakhon Pathom, west of

Bangkok. The Dvaravati kingdom flourished in the Chao Phraya river basin from the 6th or 7th to the 11th century. It embraced Theravada Buddhism (received via missionaries from Sri Lanka in the 8th century), and it is assumed that the Thai were initially converted to the faith through contact with the Mon. Other influences were in sculpture and temple architecture.

The second formative kingdom was that of Srivijaya, an approximate contemporary of Dvaravati which held sway in the Malay peninsula and Indonesian archipelago from the 8th to the late 13th century. This civilization moulded the early culture of southern Thailand, notably in sculpture.

The third and most influential of the pre-Thai kingdoms was that of the Khmer whose vast empire was centred on Angkor. Unlike the Mon, whose cultural dominance was never matched by their political power, the Khmer were a powerful force who by the 11th century dominated not only what is now Cambodia but also large tracts of eastern and central present-day Thailand, as well as other parts of the Indochina peninsula. They were master builders and traces of their achievements are still readily discernible in Thailand at Lopburi and various sites in the North-east, such as Phimai and Phanom Rung, where extensive ruins of Khmer temples survive.

BIRTH OF A NATION

The generally accepted theory is that Thais originated in southern China, where their formerly disparate tribal states banded together to form the kingdom of Nan Chao, in what is now China's Yunnan province. But that unity was lost in 1253, when Nan Chao was overwhelmed by the Mongol army of Kublai Khan. The effect was to accelerate migration southward into Thailand.

Certainly the Thais had firmly established themselves among the Mon and Khmer by the 13th century, setting up tiny quasi-independent fiefdoms. Then, in about 1238, the chieftains of two such Thai power groups united their forces and succeeded in pushing back the western borders of the Khmer empire and founding the first unified Thai capital at Sukhothai. One of the chieftains, Phor Khun Bang Klang Thao, was proclaimed king, taking the title Sri Intradit and establishing the first Thai dynasty, Phra Ruang. This is regarded by the Thais as marking their emergence as a distinct nation. Appropriately, the name Sukhothai translates as 'Dawn of Happiness'.

As the undisputed centre of this new Thai nation, Sukhothai reigned supreme for only 140 years. In 1378 it became a vassal of up-and-coming Ayutthaya to the south, and 60 years later it was totally absorbed by this younger Thai capital.

The 'lotus-bud' chedi *at Wat Mahathat, Sukhothai's royal temple, was erected during King Lithai's reign.*

In the first two reigns nothing disturbed the peace of the kingdom, which at the time extended little beyond the capital and the second city of Si Satchanalai some 70 kilometres (45 miles) to the north. It was in the reign of King Ramkamhaeng (c.1279–99) that Sukhothai experienced its golden age. Under his masterful leadership the kingdom was consolidated, politically through territorial gains and culturally through the adoption of Theravada Buddhism.

However, the art and architecture of the city did not reach their apogee until around the mid 14th century. At that time, during the reign of King Lithai (1347–c.68), a man noted for his religious conviction and scholarship, Theravada Buddhism was strengthened through direct links with Sri Lanka. In consequence the building of *chedis* and other religious structures was accelerated and it was now that the 'lotus-bud' *chedi*, characterized by a bulbous dome at the top of the spire and unique to Sukhothai architecture, made its appearance.

The economy of Sukhothai was as equally developed as its cultural achievements. Although the economic base was rice cultivation, supplemented by fishing in the rivers and streams, commerce in both fresh produce and Sukhothai's own distinctive ceramic wares thrived, generating trade contacts with, among others, China, Burma (now Myanmar), Sri Lanka, Java and Persia.

As a city influencing the development of a nation's art, culture and economy, Sukhothai thrived only briefly. Like one of its festive candles, it burned bright, then flickered and was extinguished. In 1438 the Phra Ruang dynasty came to an end and Sukhothai was ruled by an Ayutthaya prince. Then, probably at the end of the 15th century or the beginning of the 16th, the city was finally abandoned.

Founded by King U Thong (later crowned Ramathibodi) in 1350, Ayutthaya rapidly gained power and, after absorbing Sukhothai, remained the heart of the Thai state for the next 400 years. Situated at the junction of the Chao Phraya, Lopburi and Pa Sak rivers, it was created as an island city and its network of communication canals set the pattern of riverine settlement that typifies Thai communities.

Quickly superseding Sukhothai, Ayutthaya took over the role of religious, cultural and commercial capital of the Thais, and the city was later to serve as the model for Bangkok. At the height of its power in the 17th century, Ayutthaya, exercising control over nearly all of Thailand except the North, was one of the most magnificent cities in the Orient. The city walls enclosed palaces, hundreds of temples and separate quarters for the military, scholars, artists and artisans. Outside the walls were the settlements, or 'factories' as they were known, of various foreign communities,

French, Dutch and British, as well as Asian.

From the start, Ayutthaya went from strength to strength and by the end of the 14th century it was the strongest power in South-east Asia. In addition to what is now Thai territory, Ayutthaya came to rule over parts of Laos and Cambodia. Its might was not unchallenged, however, and in the 16th century Burma rose to become a powerful and constant threat, and succeeded in capturing the city in 1569. With their typical resilience, the Thais rose from the ashes, although steady, if periodic, warfare with Burma dominated Ayutthaya's foreign affairs throughout most of its history.

The full flowering of Ayutthaya's glory, its cultural achievements and its wealth, as well as power, came in the 17th century and was based on trade. The Thais themselves were not great merchants – the common people were farmers, the nobles administrators – but they permitted others to carry on trade under a royal monopoly.

With China and Japan effectively closed to outsiders, Ayutthaya became a major entrepôt for the expanding East-West trade. First, in 1511, came the Portuguese, then the Dutch in 1605, the English in 1612 and the Danes in 1621. The French, eventually to have great, albeit ill-fated and short-lived, influence at court, arrived in 1662.

SEVENTEENTH-CENTURY INTRIGUE

As a centre of international interest, Ayutthaya came into its own in the reign of King Narai (1656–88). It and the city of Lopburi, which Narai used as a second capital, were where one of the most thrilling episodes in Thai history was played out.

King Narai ranks as one of the greatest Thai monarchs and his long reign presents a fine record of achievements, though he is most noted for an ambitious policy that ultimately failed. His rule coincided with the culmination of the first big wave of European interest in South-east Asia, and he was determined to reap benefits while safeguarding his nation's sovereignty by playing off the

Dutch against the English and the French against the Dutch in order to foil any one power gaining ascendancy.

For a while his policies seemed as if they would meet with success. He attracted Westerners to come and trade with Siam and he fitted out his own ships, usually with foreign crews, to trade with India, Persia, China and Japan. Many of the Westerners taken into royal service were adventurers, like the swashbuckling Englishman, Samuel White, one-time Narai's harbour master at Mergui, whose main concern was that of lining their own pockets.

The one foreigner who played a leading role at this moment of Ayutthaya's history was, however, a more complex character. Phaulkon, as he was known, was a Greek born with the family name Gerakis ('falcon') Constantine who ran away to sea as a boy. He eventually came to the Orient on a vessel of the British East India Company and with the help of British friends set himself up as a trader at Ayutthaya.

An amazingly resourceful man, driven by powerful ambition, he soon attracted the attention of King Narai. He entered government service in 1680 and from 1683 until his death five years later he was the king's first minister and the principal go-between

Adventurous Westerners and foreign envoys thronged to King Narai's fine palace at Lopburi.

during the first diplomatic exchanges between France and Siam. During the height of his career Phaulkon wielded incredible power and influence, amassing enormous wealth and living in opulence.

The mainspring of events focusing on Phaulkon was King Narai's fear of Dutch commercial and colonial intentions in the region and his desire to balance their power by courting another European faction. In turning to the French, at the time the all-powerful nation in Europe, Phaulkon was simply pursuing the earlier policies of his adopted king as, in 1680, Narai had already sent a first Siamese mission to Paris, though it never arrived and was presumed lost at sea.

Despite further diplomatic exchanges with the court of Louis XIV, a Franco-Siamese relationship did not prosper. In simple terms Narai wanted military aid as a deterrent to whatever designs the Dutch might have, and the French desired trade concessions. In addition to port facilities and favourable commercial terms, France was also motivated by a desire to convert Narai to Catholicism.

Phaulkon was condemned for conniving with the French in their totally unrealistic religious aim. Certainly he championed their interests, though arguably only for political expediency. Perhaps over-confident, he attempted to walk an impossible diplomatic tightrope. What he may have achieved in terms of international relations will never be known; he was overtaken by events. On his way to the second most powerful position in the land he had made numerous enemies, none greater than General Phetracha and his son Luang Surasak, for long vicious personal antagonists.

In 1688 King Narai was dying at Lopburi; Phetracha, seeing his opportunity, led a palace revolt, murdered Narai's possible successors and took control of the nation. Called to the palace at Lopburi, Phaulkon was captured by the rebels. He was imprisoned and tortured for several days before being beheaded in a squalid nighttime execution.

The French were subsequently unceremoniously expelled from the country and Phetracha became king on the death of Narai a few weeks after Phaulkon's execution. The dynastic change effectively closed Thailand to any significant foreign relations until the mid 19th century. The nation once again became introspective and was weakened by internal squabbles. In 1767 that perennial enemy, Burma, made an all-out attack and after a lengthy siege captured Ayutthaya, looted it, killed or took off into slavery all but 10,000 inhabitants and razed the city. It was the end of an era.

Ferocious though the Burmese attack was, the invaders were unable to consolidate territorial gains. The Thais were quickly rallied under General Taksin, who had established a resistance base at Thonburi on the opposite bank of the Chao Phraya river from Bangkok. Before the close of the year Taksin had established a new capital, had been crowned king and had begun to reunite the people. Within 15 years Thailand would be revitalized, poised to launch itself into the modern era.

THE KINGDOM OF THE NORTH

The mainstream history of Thailand is that of Sukhothai and Ayutthaya, but for most of the period covered by these two kingdoms, a parallel Thai state remained independent in the North. Known as Lanna, this kingdom was a contemporary of Sukhothai and later held out against the power of Ayutthaya.

Northern Thailand today is a popular tourist destination and draws at least part of its charm from a distinct character of its own. Topographically different from the Central Plains and Chao Phraya basin where Sukhothai and Ayutthaya rose to power, the region is an area of high hills cut through by river valleys running north to south. This distinction of geography is important. While Sukhothai could be comparatively easily absorbed by the more powerful Ayutthaya in the 15th century, Lanna, protected by physical barriers, could defend its autonomy and resist integration into the Thai nation proper until much later.

The earliest inhabitants of the North were probably the Lawa, or Lue, who lived for centuries in the valleys until they were forced up into the highlands where, in greatly reduced numbers, they continue to

One of King Narai's three ambassadors, who were received at the court of Louis XIV of France in 1686.

survive as one of the major hilltribes. Supplanting the Lawa was a group of Mon, an offshoot of the Mon kingdom of Dvaravati centred in the Chao Phraya river basin near what is now Bangkok. They were led by a legendary queen, Chama Devi, who founded her capital in AD 660 at Haripunchai, present-day Lamphun, located 25 kilometres (15 miles) south of Chiang Mai.

Controlling the Chiang Mai valley and the Ping river, respectively the most fertile land in the area and the major communication link, Haripunchai long dominated the area. But gradually some of the Thais who migrated south from China began to settle in the area and set up petty city states. By the 13th century the most powerful of these was Chiang Saen, on the banks of the Mekong river, across the mountains northeast of the Chiang Mai valley.

In 1259, King Mengrai succeeded his father as the ruler of Chiang Saen. A man of ambition and determination, he saw that neighbouring Thai principalities were frequently in conflict with one another, and decided to impose his authority over the entire region. He acted swiftly and, in quick

succession, took nearby states before driving south to set up a temporary capital at Chiang Rai in 1262.

Mengrai had done well, but Chiang Rai was not a good strategic base. The terrain is rugged and hampers easy territorial expansion. Mengrai had yet to conquer natural barriers. In 1274 he made a major breakthrough and crossed westwards over the mountains to Fang, due north of Chiang Mai. This still did not give him control of the Chiang Mai valley and the plum of his conquests, Haripunchai, remained to be picked.

This was a different proposition from the weak little principalities he had so far conquered. It was extremely powerful and not easy to lead a large army against as the surrounding countryside would have been densely forested. So Mengrai's advisors warned him that the Mon kingdom would fall only to guile. He acted accordingly, planting spies in the city and biding his time until circumstances gave him victory with little opposition.

After seizing the throne of Haripunchai, Mengrai was de facto ruler of a state he was to call Lanna, meaning the kingdom of 'a million rice fields'. Seeing the fertile Chiang Mai valley today, which yields nearly half a million tons of rice a year, it is still easy to imagine how appropriate the name was.

Mengrai decided not to install himself at Haripunchai and instead set up yet another temporary base at Kum Kam, not far from the site of Chiang Mai. The question of a capital worthy of his kingdom, however, could not be postponed indefinitely.

It was in 1291, so legend has it, that Mengrai was out hunting one day and passed by the banks of the Ping river. At one spot he sighted a pair of white sambar deer, a pair of white barking deer and a white mouse with five young. The appearance of such a notable collection of creatures was deemed auspicious. Mengrai immediately halted his caravan and decided that here, a short distance west of the river, he would build his capital.

Anxious to construct a city that would reflect the glory of the Lanna kingdom, Mengrai consulted his two powerful allies, the kings of Phayao and Sukhothai, over the design. The three of them worked out plans for a rectangular walled settlement measuring 2 kilometres by 1.6 kilometres (1¼ x 1 mile). It was to be called Nopphaburi Si Nakhonping Chiangmai which, in its use of both Sanskrit and Thai words, is an oddly repetitive name that translates roughly as 'new city, city of the Ping, new city'. When building finally began in 1296, it is believed that some 90,000 workers were involved.

Mengrai died in 1317, reputedly struck by lightning. Thus ended a remarkable reign that had spanned nearly 60 years and had brought much of what is now northern Thailand into one fold, Lanna, with Chiang Mai as its power base. Immediate successors were kings of lesser stature and there were some troubled times as the state was weakened by internal squabbles. Nevertheless, a vital boost to political and cultural identity was achieved in the reign of King Ku Na (1355–85). He was a man of learning as well as an accomplished administrator and he invited a much-respected monk from Sukhothai, the Venerable Sumana, to establish his order of Singhalese Buddhism in Chiang Mai.

While Chiang Mai continued to grow, the power of Lanna became such as to attract the hostile interest of fast-expanding Ayutthaya. However, partly because the northern terrain inhibited military expeditions, Chiang Mai was never permanently defeated. A see-saw kind of conflict, with fleeting triumphs by either side but never a conclusive victory, became the pattern in relations between Lanna and Ayutthaya from the mid 15th century onwards.

None of this prevented Chiang Mai from experiencing its golden age during the reign of King Tilokaraja (1442–87). A formidable warrior, he was a worthy opponent of Ayutthaya's equally forceful King Trailok. The history of the period is a thrilling one and the tales of successive military campaigns in which each king tried to outwit the other make exciting reading.

Lanna was conquered by the Burmese in 1557 and for the next two centuries Chiang Mai was subjugated. The form of the eclipse was erratic; sometimes there were puppet Lanna kings, at other times there was direct rule from Burma, and various principalities occasionally made a bid for independence, while Ayutthaya was never completely out of the picture.

This state of affairs persisted until the late 18th century when an ambitious young

A royal garden was chosen as the site for Wat Suan Dok, Chiang Mai. Here at the back of the temple compound lie tombs of the royal family of Lanna, the kingdom of the North.

general, Taksin, forced the Burmese out of the North as well as the rest of the country. Reconstruction of the North now began although the region, while part of the Thai fold, retained a certain autonomy under a line of hereditary rulers until the early 20th century when there was direct rule in all spheres from the central government.

EMERGENCE OF THE MODERN STATE
While Taksin, proclaimed king and ruling from his capital at Thonburi, had led the Thais to a remarkable recovery from the Burmese invasion and largely reunified the nation, including, for the first time, the northern regions, his reign was short-lived. By 1782 he was showing increasing signs of megalomania and became alienated from the people who, faced with a deteriorating situation, called on army commander General Chakri to solve the problem.

By the time Chakri returned from a military expedition in Laos, King Taksin had reputedly become insane and was executed. The army commander was popularly proclaimed king, being crowned Rama I and

thus founding the Chakri dynasty which reigns to this day. One of his first acts was to transfer his power-base across the Chao Phraya from Thonburi to Bangkok, at the time little more than a customs post and a huddle of Chinese traders' huts.

Throughout Rama I's reign and that of his two successors Bangkok was transformed from a sleepy riverside village into a metropolis that replicated the lost glory of Ayutthaya as faithfully as possible. The construction of canals effectively turned it into an island city, while the building of the Grand Palace, the Temple of the Emerald Buddha and the other classical monuments that today constitute Bangkok's major sights reflected a material and spiritual wealth worthy of the capital's status.

During the first three reigns of the Chakri dynasty Thailand restored the cultural heritage that had been fragmented by the destruction of Ayutthaya. The country also set about an aggressive expansionist policy, taking the western provinces of Cambodia and claiming suzerainty over other neighbouring territories.

With the succession in 1851 of King Mongkut, Rama IV – best known, if distortedly so, to the West through the musical *The King and I* – there was a radical shift of emphasis. The idea of recreating Ayutthaya was abandoned along with the nation's introspective stance. Regional expansionism was halted and was replaced by a more internationalist policy, with the nation looking to the outside world, especially the West, for ways in which to modernize.

Not since the ill-fated French embassies of the late 1680s had Thailand made overtures to the outside world and encouraged foreign interests. That was to change in 1855 when King Mongkut abolished the royal trade monopoly and signed a mutually favourable treaty of friendship and commerce with Britain's Sir John Bowring, envoy of Queen Victoria. Similar accords with other European countries and with the United States of America soon followed.

International trade grew steadily from the mid 19th century onwards and the country embarked upon a programme of modernization of far-reaching proportions. Infrastructure was expanded and developed to meet new needs (notably roads for wheeled traffic began to replace canals), and the machinery of state was overhauled with ministries organized more along European lines.

Mongkut's eldest son and successor, Chulalongkorn, King Rama V (reigned 1868–1910), vastly furthered the policies of modernization. He successfully introduced various far-sighted reforms, the abolition of slavery among them, and broadly adopted European concepts of administration, justice, education and public welfare.

On the international front, Chulalongkorn maintained extremely cordial relations with European monarchs. He wisely realized Thailand was not in a position to exert force against any foreign territorial designs, and instead sought to create a state of equilibrium between contending powers.

The pattern of enlightened modernization persisted in the following reign of Vajiravudh, Rama VI (1910–25). He was the first Thai monarch to be educated overseas (in England) and, among other initiatives, he established compulsory education, as well as fostering a heightened sense of nationalism. With respect to foreign policy, he brought Thailand into World War I on the side of the allies.

In the wake of economic change and material development it was almost inevitable that traditional concepts of power would be questioned. For centuries Thai kings had been literally 'Lords of Life', but by the late 1920s Vajiravudh's successor, King Prajadhipok (1925–35), was considering ways to liberalize the system. Events, however, influenced considerably by shocks in the world economy, overtook him. In 1932 a bloodless revolution, organized by middle-level civil servants and military officers, changed the system of government to a constitutional monarchy. Prajadhipok accepted a *fait accompli* though he abdicated in 1935 and lived until his death six years later as a self-imposed exile in England. His nephew, Ananda, still in his minority, then ascended the throne as Rama VIII.

NEW DIRECTIONS

The coup of 1932 was directed primarily against the ministers of the conservative government, rather than against the person of the king. None the less its immediate result was to share the rule which was formerly the king's alone between three emerging power groups: civil servants, the military and the merchant class. During the initial period of constitutional monarchy two figures dominated the political scene – the progressive Dr Pridi Banomyong, a lawyer, and Major Luang Pibulsongkhram, a young army officer. A power struggle resulted in the eventual ascendancy of Major Pibulsongkhram, and during the 1940s and 1950s Thailand struggled uneasily through a period of right-wing nationalism in which the government attempted to forge a new national identity. Essentially nationalism was equated with Westernization, although it was neither politically nor culturally pro-

In 1782 Rama I entered Bangkok (top) to establish it as his capital. By 1890, foreign visitors filled the city's still renowned Oriental Hotel (above).

Western. During World War II the Thai government acquiesced in the Japanese occupation of the country, although the Thai minister in Washington refused to deliver his country's declaration of war on the United States and instead set about organizing a Free Thai movement.

In the post-war years Thailand has moved slowly and, at times, with difficulty, towards establishing an effective democracy. Since 1932 there have been nearly 30 prime ministers and the constitution has undergone numerous changes and revisions. The role of the military has been strong and some 16 coups, successful and abortive, have to varying degrees disturbed the peaceful evolution of government.

Throughout, the monarchy, albeit constitutional, has had a valuable stabilizing effect. King Ananda was tragically killed in the palace in 1946 under circumstances that have never been made clear and was succeeded by his brother, the present King Bhumibol Adulyadej, Rama IX.

A man of considerable personal accomplishment, King Bhumibol has shown himself to be the model of a modern constitutional monarch, both preserving regal traditions and taking an active part in working towards the greater social and economic well-being of his people. The people's respect and love for the monarchy is as great today as ever.

THAILAND TODAY

In the 1990s, Thailand made gains towards greater democracy. The threat of military coups, although not entirely vanished, has significantly receded. None the less, a profusion of political parties, along with a tradition of power through patronage rather than ability, still tend to inhibit sustained policy implementation. The economy, on the other hand, has gone from strength to strength, until halted by recession in mid-1997. Prior to that the country experienced an unprecedented boom that started in the late 1980s. During those years double-figure economic growth was spearheaded by a dynamic export drive. Agriculture, the traditional source of income, remained strong enough to ensure Thailand's position as a world-ranking food exporter. Its performance, however, was outstripped by manufacturing. Today, not only does the world buy most of its rice, tapioca and tinned pineapples from the Kingdom; it is also increasingly shopping for made-in-Thailand shoes, garments, jewellery and other manufactured items. Increased exports and an enhanced profile in the international arena, combined with a pool of inexpensive labour and other incentives, further served to promote the Kingdom as an investment centre.

The third leg of the country's sturdy economic stool is the service industry and nothing quite matches the success of tourism, today's single largest money-spinner. A 'Visit Thailand Year' promotion brought in a then record 3.5 million visitors in 1987. Subsequently, an 'Amazing Thailand' campaign in 1998/99 boosted arrivals beyond the 7 million mark, and tourism growth continues.

A crucial factor in Thailand's recent success has been stability. The economy has enjoyed stability through being resilient, broad-based and diversified. Political stability was boosted during the steadying premiership of Prem Tinsulanonda, who held the top government post from 1980 to 1988; and comparative social

stability springs from what is probably the region's most homogeneous society, moulded by enduring traditions and long-held values.

Thailand is not, of course, problem-free and the recession years of the late 1990s have promoted much rethinking, particularly over problems in the banking and finance sectors. Presently such difficulties affect mostly Bangkok, though that in itself is indicative of another problem – decentralization, or rather the lack of it. Historically the capital has always been the centre of all major activity, but in the current economic climate demands that what is almost a city-state concept must change. Moreover, a greater proportion of the increasing wealth needs be channelled to the country's poorer rural areas. At present annual per-capita income in Bangkok is nearly three times greater than the national average.

Certain provincial districts, however, have not escaped latter-day difficulties. Tourism development has been rapid, too rapid in some places, and while it has brought great benefits to the traveller in terms of both access and facilities, largely unplanned development is having a detrimental effect on the environment.

Fortunately, there are signs of a growing awareness for the need to change and to balance the pursuit of material prosperity with consideration for the greater good of the nation.

PEOPLES OF THAILAND

Thailand is home to a population now topping 60 million, of which slightly more than 10 per cent lives in Bangkok. Unlike many other Asian countries, Thailand has never suffered from over-population, neither in the modern age nor historically; a fact which has contributed to the nation's relative prosperity.

The country is still evolving from its traditional agrarian base and the rural village tied to the agricultural cycle remains an important social unit. Bangkok, with a population of at least seven million, is by far the largest city and the biggest provincial towns – Khon Kaen, Chiang Mai, Khorat, Hat Yai – each scarcely number more than a few hundred thousand inhabitants.

The overwhelming majority of Thais are Tai, the distinction being between citizens of Thailand and people who belong to the Tai ethnic group. Ostensibly, Thailand displays a marked ethnic and linguistic homogeneity. More than 80 per cent of the population speaks related dialects belonging to the Tai language group. The social structure is, however, more complex than it first seems. The apparent and, in political terms, real homogeneity is the result of cultural hegemony of the Central Thai over the other Tai peoples who live within the national boundaries. Basically there are four Thai groups: central Thai, northern Thai, southern Thai and the Thai-Lao of the north-east. A number of small subgroupings, such as the Lue peoples of the North, further contribute to what is a complex human fabric, although centuries of harmonious co-mingling have blurred the finer distinctions beyond all recognition for all but the anthropologist.

More enduring differences have resulted from Thailand having in the past been subject to various migratory patterns, and so Chinese, Malay, Mon, Khmer, Burmese and Indian ethnic strains are found in varying degrees. There is no clearly defined pattern to the mix, although, for example, roughly half of Bangkok's population is of at least partial Chinese descent, while the southern Thais display certain Malay characteristics. Such influences are historical and today assimilation of the principal minorities is almost total.

Tourism is Thailand's largest industry. For the visitor the country has everything to offer: glittering temples, tropical beaches and a wealth of culture and tradition. Here, dancers relax after a cultural show.

The different hill peoples of the North are most readily recognized by their distinctive attire. Most flamboyant of all are the Akha women whose unique headdresses (right), laden with silver coins and balls, are still commonly worn. The somewhat more reserved female costume of the Yao (far right) comprises an elegant turban, crimson boa, tunic, cummerbund and patterned trousers.

THE CHINESE

Among the non-Tai peoples it is the Chinese who have had the most profound impact in terms of social and economic prominence. Although Chinese immigrants had settled in Thailand since the Ayutthaya period, and probably earlier, it was only in the 19th century, following the founding of the Chakri dynasty and the creation of Bangkok as the capital, that they began arriving in significant numbers. Between 1825 and 1910, the Chinese population in Bangkok rose from around 230,000 to 792,000. More important than just the size of the community were the roles the Chinese filled. The Bowring Treaty of 1855 led to a vast expansion of trade and commerce, and it was the Chinese who came to fill the essential roles of labourers and middlemen. It is only today that an emerging Thai middle class is beginning to make any inroads into the world of finance and commerce.

The most surprising fact has been the assimilation of the Chinese into Thai society. People of Chinese origin are not only Thai nationals, they have adopted Thai surnames and speak Thai, even if they may still converse in their local dialects at home – they are to all intents and purposes Thai.

This was not always the case, and in the early decades of the 20th century Bangkok was to an extent a city of two nations, Thai and Chinese, and harmonious relations did not always prevail. However, government pressure towards assimilation, aided by an increasing rate of intermarriage, eventually brought the two races together in a way that differences ceased to exist in any practical sense. Chinese customs survive, most notably in the celebration of Chinese New Year, and cultural distinctions are still visible in Bangkok's Chinatown but, unlike similar enclaves in other South-east Asia cities, the Chinese quarter is merely a historical remnant and not a focal point to which citizens of Chinese descent cling with any sense of national identity. Today, ethnic Chinese are found throughout Bangkok and everywhere in the country.

THE HILL PEOPLES

Inhabiting the highlands of northern and western Thailand are groups of hill peoples, ethnic minorities who constitute some dozen different 'tribes', ranging in size from the Karen who number more than 200,000, to the Phi Thong Luang, 'Spirits of the Yellow Leaves', of whom only a few score survive. The total population of hill peoples has been estimated at around 550,000.

Linguistically the tribes fall into three broad categories: Tibetan-Burman, which includes the Karen, Akha, Lisu, Lahu and Kachin; Mon-Khmer, comprising Soai, Tin and several smaller groups such as the Lue; and the Miao-Yao, of which there are two main groups, both originally from China – the Hmong (as they call themselves, Miao in Chinese and Meo in Thai), and the Yao. All are distinguished by their own languages, religious beliefs (mostly animistic), customs and tribal dress typically featuring elaborate embroidery and silver jewellery, the latter constituting the family wealth.

Pursuing a mainly semi-nomadic existence, most of the hilltribes migrated to Thailand from Tibet, Burma, China and Laos during the last 100–200 years. The earliest tribal people, however, likely established a presence in the northern part of the country during the Dvaravati period, while the latest arrivals, the Yao, mostly migrated from Laos only after 1945.

While some tribespeople are moving to the lowlands and mingling with the Thai population, most continue to live outside mainstream society and carry on traditional independent lifestyles in the jungle-covered mountain slopes of the border areas. Cultivation of the opium poppy by some hill peoples, but by no means all, along with environmentally destructive swidden (slash-and-burn) farming methods has served to focus government attention on the hilltribes in recent years. In an effort to raise living standards and alleviate deep-rooted prob-

All over Thailand, Buddhist monks make early morning alms rounds (left), *receiving food and other offerings. The monastic life is lived in temple communities, such as that adjacent to Wat Phra That Haripunchai, Lamphun* (right). *Many monks are ordained for three months only.*

Written Thai has evolved from a south Indian script via Mon and Khmer writing, and with only slight modifications, the alphabet which was formalized in the late 13th century has survived in modern Thai, which consists of 44 consonants and 32 vowels. Writing reads from left to right but words are not separated within sentences and punctuation is minimal.

CULTURE AND BELIEFS

lems – poverty, drugs and environmentally destructive agricultural practices – a number of government and Royal projects have been instigated. Most are aimed at education and cash crop substitution programmes, the latter having notable effect in reducing the extent of opium cultivation.

LANGUAGE
What is known as 'standard Thai', the national language taught in schools and used in all forms of written and spoken address, as well as by the media, is the language of the Central Thai. People in other parts of the country speak their own dialects and, to a greater or lesser extent hold to regional customs. The differences do not now create any significant division and are largely indistinguishable to the non-Thai-speaking outsider.

Thai is a tonal language which makes it hard for Westerners to learn. There are five tones – even, high, low, rising and falling – and so one word, depending on how it is sounded, may have five different meanings. To all but the most acute ear the different pronunciations may sound identical.

The language has had a diverse evolution, developing from a Chinese-influenced, tonal, monosyllabic language first through borrowings from Mon and Khmer words. Later, from contact with Brahmanism and Theravada Buddhism, the Thais absorbed polysyllabic words from Sanskrit and Pali.

BUDDHISM
Throughout the Kingdom's 700-year history Buddhism has been Thailand's national religion. It was the faith under which the people were first united, and ever since it has served, together with the monarchy, as the most important cohesive force in Thai society, underpinning the entire culture. Today, Buddhism remains vital and visible in daily life, not only professed but practised by nine-tenths of the population.

Essentially Buddhism is a way of life, a rational philosophy based on seeing, knowing, understanding and accepting worldly reality. It derives from the teachings of the Buddha, the 'Enlightened One', the title of a historical person who lived more than 2,500 years ago.

Named Siddhartha Gautama, the Buddha was born around 560 BC near present-day Lumbini, southern Nepal. He was the son of a king and grew up in his father's palace amid ease and luxury. One day, curiosity led him outside the palace, where he was shocked to see examples of disease, old age and death.

Prince Siddhartha's exposure to misery made him determined to find a way to save mankind from suffering. He accordingly left his wife and child, renounced the riches of his birth and became an ascetic. After six years' wandering he abandoned the extreme form of asceticism he had been following, electing instead a 'Middle Way' of moder-

ation and meditation. It was while meditating, reputedly seated beneath a bo tree in the vicinity of Bodh Gaya, northern India, that he attained enlightenment, supreme understanding of man's predicament.

Implicit in this understanding is a belief in the earlier Indian concept of reincarnation. Thus the ultimate aim of Buddhism is the release from the endless cycle of rebirth and suffering by extinguishing desire, which is to achieve the state of *nirvana*.

The Buddha spent his long life teaching around the central region of the Ganges plain, gathering a large number of followers. Some of his disciples became ordained and formed the monkhood (*sangha*) in which they lived disciplined lives and sought wisdom, their prime virtue.

The early form of Buddhism, known as Theravada or the 'teaching of the elders', was later challenged by a new school with a more popular appeal. It called itself Mahayana, or 'Great Vehicle' as it offered salvation to a greater number of people than Theravada Buddhism, which it derisively termed Hinayana, or 'Small Vehicle'.

The Mahayana school places less emphasis on monasticism and claims any layman might achieve *nirvana*. It also differs in considering the Buddha omnipresent, representing not only the Enlightened One but also the principle of Enlightenment. Mahayana further introduces the concept of the Bodhisattvas, Enlightened beings who declined entering *nirvana* in order to help others.

Buddhism was first introduced to the region that is now Thailand in the 3rd century BC when, according to tradition, the Indian emperor Ashoka sent two missionaries to the 'Land of Gold'. This has been tentatively identified as the Mon kingdom of Dvaravati centred on the modern town of Nakhon Pathom, west of Bangkok.

By the time of the founding of the first Thai sovereign state at Sukhothai in the early 13th century, Buddhist monks in the southern part of the country had made contact with Sri Lanka. From there came the doctrine of Theravada Buddhism based on Pali texts, as opposed to the Sanskrit scriptures of Mahayana.

Today, Thailand supports a religious community of some 250,000 monks who reside at an estimated 27,000 temple monasteries throughout the country. The monastic system is central to Theravada Buddhism and, aside from a core religious community, most monks are ordained for only a short spell, perhaps just a few days but more usually the three months of the Buddhist Rains Retreat. As in the past, young Thai men become monks temporarily to earn merit for their parents as well as for their own spiritual development.

In trying to lead a good life the layman, too, has the opportunity to accrue merit which will ensure rebirth under more favourable conditions in the next incarnation. Ways in which lay people may earn merit are many and various. Most typical and most visible is giving food and other offerings to monks who make early morning alms rounds in cities, towns, and villages throughout the country.

OTHER RELIGIONS

Although Thais are overwhelmingly Buddhist, they are a tolerant people and other religions coexist with the national faith. Muslims comprise Thailand's largest religious minority, numbering about 2 million, or roughly 4 per cent of the population. Islam was reputedly introduced into the region in the 13th century by Arab traders calling at ports along the Malay peninsula, and most Thai Muslims are of Malay descent, living primarily in the southernmost provinces of Narathiwat, Pattani, Yala and Satun. Aside from Thailand's approximately 2,000 mosques and some 200 Muslim schools, freedom to practise the faith is witnessed in many ways and, for example, government employees are allowed leave to attend major festivals, as well as to make the Haj pilgrimage.

A further 1 per cent of Thailand's population is made up of Christians, Taoists, Mahayana Buddhists, Confucianists, Hindus

Robed in white, to represent purity, and bearing a traditional offering, a young man is carried, shoulder-high, to the temple for his ordination as a monk.

and Sikhs. The practice of these faiths largely follows ethnic patterns, and there have been comparatively few Thai converts. Ethnic Chinese and Vietnamese account for most of the Christians, Taoists, Mahayana Buddhists and Confucianists, while Hindus and Sikhs belong mainly to Bangkok's sizeable Indian community.

While other minority religions owe their presence primarily to migration, Christianity was brought to Thailand by missionaries. First, in the 16th and 17th centuries, came Dominicans, Franciscans and Jesuits from Spain and Portugal, and later they were joined by their Protestant counterparts, Presbyterians, Baptists and Seventh-Day Adventists. In spite of making few converts among the Thais, Christianity has had a significant impact, especially in education and medicine. Many local schools and hospitals are Christian affiliated, while Western surgery, vaccination and other medical practices were first introduced by Christians.

THE SUPERNATURAL

Pervasive and genuine though their adherence to Buddhism is, the Thais have inherited from their ancestors animistic practices which interact with ordinary life. These include beliefs in charms, amulets, magical tattoos, fortune-telling, exorcism and other shamanistic rituals, as well as in spirits.

Buddhism, in placing ultimate responsibility for salvation firmly on each individual, does not address in any practical way people's fears and hopes as encountered in day-to-day life. Accordingly, the Thais have retained a host of ancient beliefs in supernatural forces which are thought to be capable of influencing and exerting power over the events of daily life. The beliefs originated with the human mind's attempt to cope with the uncontrollable crises of mundane existence – accidents, natural disasters, disease and other sources of fear and insecurity.

Perhaps the most widespread and easily seen manifestations of supernatural beliefs are spirit houses. Found in the compounds of virtually every home, business premises, government office and public building, these are ornate model dwellings designed in the form of temples or traditional-style Thai houses. Commonly raised on a short column, they are usually garlanded with flowers and often provided with food offerings. Their presence stems from a belief that spirits inhabited the site before humans settled in and, lest they should become angered and bring misfortune, they must be placated by the provision of a home of their own.

More troublesome than the spirits inhabiting a compound are others which can take possession of a person's body. To combat these there is a variety of shamans and exorcists, mostly lay people but sometimes monks, who are renowned for having power over malevolent *phi*, or spirits.

The act of exorcism differs from shaman to shaman. Some are extremely theatrical, favouring elaborate costumes and wielding swords and knives in their struggle to wrest the spirit from the body of the possessed. Others are less dramatic and generally employ the elements of fire and water, waving a bunch of lighted candles and sprinkling the affected subject with water.

Closely allied to exorcists are mediums, people, often women, capable of going into a trance and allowing themselves to become possessed by a benevolent spirit. Under this influence they are able to perform acts of healing and similar services.

While shamans and mediums perform a curative function, tattoos and amulets play a prophylactic role in supernatural belief. Both are thought to bestow invulnerability from all kinds of weapons, also to protect against snake bites, as well as to give the power of attracting admiration and love.

Tattoo designs are typically animals (double-tailed lizards are popular), figures from classical Thai mythology or magic spells written in ancient Khmer script. Amulets can be all manner of things. Most common are images of the Buddha or some highly revered monk. However, as amulets long pre-date Buddhism, and were initially rare objects found in nature – a hollow tiger's tooth, for example – many have no religious association. Popular among these are wooden phalluses, *palad khik*, and small rolls of gilded metal containing a magic inscription, *takrud*.

The important thing about both tattoos and amulets is that they have no protective power in themselves, or that their power is dormant unless activated. Thus amulets must be blessed, and tattoos have a spell cast over them by the tattooist. After completing a tattoo and chanting a magic spell to imbue it with power, the tattooist will proffer moral advice. Should the tattooee not follow this and commit some sin, the power of the tattoo can be diminished or completely destroyed.

One major difference between amulets and tattoos today is that something of a social stigma is attached to the latter. Because of this some tattoos are executed in invisible ink, made from sesame oil, so the wearer may have the protective benefit without the visual marks.

FOOD AND DRINK

As an ever-growing number of restaurants around the world attest, Thai cuisine today enjoys unprecedented popularity among lovers of good food. Its distinctive blend of flavours and ingredients make it quite different from anything else in Asia.

The basis of a Thai meal is, of course, rice. This is commonly steamed, although it may be made into noodles, while glutinous or 'sticky' rice is preferred with some regional specialities. Accompanying are four or five main dishes featuring vegetables, meat, seafood, fish, egg and soup.

Besides the rice and main dishes, absolutely essential to any Thai meal are the sauces to give additional spice and seasoning. For the novice there can be a bewildering number of these, but the most common are *nam pla*, a liquid fish sauce which is extremely salty, and *nam prik*, also a liquid but with pieces of chillies, garlic, shrimp curd, sugar and lime.

Although Thais generally prefer hot, spicy food, it is a misconception that all Thai dishes are equally fiery. There are grades of hotness, and hence the array of sauces to adjust seasoning according to preference. However, much of the appeal of Thai cuisine is derived from its seasoning. Red and green chillies of a dozen kinds are but some of many different ingredients that are combined to give a unique blend of flavours. Lemon grass, garlic, ginger, nutmeg, cloves coriander, turmeric and other herbs and spices all have a role to play.

Another crucial element is the prepara-

Spirit houses, here displayed for sale, are found in the vicinity of almost every home and business throughout the country.

tion of ingredients. Thai cooks are expert in the handling of tools and skilled at slicing, cutting and carving vegetables, fruit and meats. The practice of carving food items in delicate and intricate patterns, as well as in figurative forms such as boats, fish, ornamental jars and so on, has a long tradition in Thailand. In former times this was primarily a speciality of the women at the royal court, who would turn cucumbers, papayas, tomatoes, carrots, radishes, onions and other prosaic foods into exquisite works of art fit to decorate a king's banquet table.

A further consideration for the Thai cook is time. The preparation of a Thai dinner can take all day, starting in the early morning with shopping at the local market for the day's freshest and best buys. Then the spices must be prepared anew for each meal, and ground painstakingly to ensure the perfect blend and the fullest flavour.

And so to the individual types of dishes. In the soup department, Thailand's great contribution to the culinary arts is *tom yam*. This is a sour soup which can be made with various kinds of meat or fish, but its most famous version is with prawns (*tom yam goong*). The basic broth is flavoured with lemon grass, citrus leaves, lime juice, fish sauce and hot chillies.

Other common methods of Thai food preparation include curries (*gaeng*), usually hot and spicy, and the stir-fried dishes which are cooked in a wok with pork fat oil, pepper and plenty of garlic. Then there is a wide choice of salad preparations (*yam*) made with just vegetables or with different kinds of meat or fish mixed with distinctive flavourings such as lemon grass, fish sauce and such like, plus lime juice to give a characteristic sourness. For dessert there are many sorts of local sweets (*kanom*) often of a coconut flavour, and a vast choice of tropical fruits from the common-or-garden pineapples and banana (numerous varieties) to exotic discoveries like the hairy rambutan and the tasty durian.

In addition to standard Thai dishes there are many regional specialities. In the North, for example, glutinous rather than plain rice is the typical staple, while curries tend to be thinner, made without the coconut milk favoured in central and southern Thailand. The northern region's proximity to neighbouring Myanmar (Burma) also accounts for

Thai food, especially 'royal' Thai cuisine, is as beautifully presented as it is delicious. Carving fruit and vegetables into intricate shapes is one of the most traditional – and impressive – presentation techniques.

some distinct dishes, such as *gaeng hang lay*, a pork curry seasoned with ginger, turmeric and tamarind.

North-eastern Thailand possesses a regional cuisine that has become extremely popular in recent years. It features a wide variety of exotic ingredients, among them frogs and grasshoppers, and uses chilli peppers to a greater degree than elsewhere in Thailand. Among typical north-eastern dishes often seen on menus today are green papaya salad (*som tam*) and spicy minced meat or chicken known as *laab*.

In the South, cooking tends to be dominated by two local ingredients found in abundance: seafood and coconut. Fish and shellfish caught off the southern shores appear more widely on menus than meat or poultry, while the coconut provides milk for thickening soups and curries, oil for frying and grated coconut meat which is used as a condiment. Cultural influences also play a part, as witnessed in Indian style curries and Indonesian *satays*.

For drinks, beer is a good (though comparatively expensive) complement to Thai food. Typically Thai are various local spirits of which 'Mekong' rice whisky is the most famous. Distilled from molasses and sticky rice in a month-long

process, 'Mekong' has a slightly coarse flavour which is an acquired taste.

SPORTS AND ENTERTAINMENT

The pervading lifestyle is strongly influenced by the Thais' particular talent for enjoyment, having a good time – *sanuk*, as it is in Thai. All languages have some words that cannot be perfectly translated because they embrace something special about the culture. *Sanuk* is the unique Thai word that means, more or less, 'to be fun' and *sanuk* is found in all things from organized entertainment to eating or simply taking a walk; *pai teeo*, roughly translating as 'taking a stroll', is the standard response to the question of 'where are you going' asked on a chance encounter in the street.

In the wake of the nation's rapid modernization and Westernization, today's Thais like to play golf, go to the cinema and eat hamburgers and fries. But even in pursuing these alien activities the people display an essentially Thai delight in anything that is new, different, novel. Golf is given a typically Thai sybaritic touch. New courses are landscaped by the dozen, clubhouses are luxurious, and caddies, usually young girls, are so cheap that a golfer may hire several, one to carry clubs, one to hold an umbrella, one to spot to the ball, one to fetch drinks and perhaps another to offer consolation at a sliced shot.

None the less traditional sports and pastimes still persist. Kick boxing (*Muay Thai*) remains Thailand's most popular spectator sport. Developed from an ancient style of martial art, *Muay Thai* differs from ordinary boxing in using the feet, knees and elbows as weapons in addition to gloved fists. At its best it is a fast and furious contest between two superbly fit athletes. Often as entertaining as the fight are the spectators who variously shout encouragement, yell abuse and gesticulate madly as bets are made across the crowded arena.

Other violent sports are Thai sword fighting (*krabi-krabong*), and improbable animal contests: bull fighting (a southern Thai speciality in which bull is pitted against bull), fish fighting, cock fighting (illegal) and even beetle fighting (two males are placed on a bamboo stick in which a female has been trapped and are made to fight for the honour).

Also very Thai but far less violent is *takraw*, a game somewhat akin to volleyball in which a rattan ball is knocked around by using the feet, legs and head only. A recognized sport at national and regional meets, *takraw* is, however, most commonly seen being played by young labourers during their lunch break on any open space

Popular with young and old alike is kite-flying, from February to May. Colourful little paper creations fill Thai skies at this time, but kite flying is also a sport, a contest in which huge *chula* 'masculine' kites try to bring down smaller *pakpao* 'female' kites.

THE VISUAL ARTS

ARCHITECTURE

Two traditional building forms define the architecture of Thailand: the Buddhist temple (from which royal and ceremonial architecture was also derived) and the teakwood

Kick boxing contests are exciting events. The pace is fast, the atmosphere charged and the noise loud. The contestants' most lethal weapons are their feet, which can be used against all parts of the body.

house. Both forms depend very largely on an architecture of the roof, with buildings being essentially post-and-beam structures supporting steeply angled, multi-tiered roofs with overhanging eaves. The basic design originates from Chinese architecture, which had a strong influence on East Asia in much the same way as ancient Greece can be said to have 'invented' architecture for the West.

Created to impart a sense of reverence and serenity, the Thai Buddhist temple is in essence a harmonious arrangement of simple horizontal masses and highly decorated vertical forms. To describe the architecture as a 'temple' is somewhat misleading as the label, implying a single structure, like a Christian church, is an unsatisfactory trans-

lation of the Thai word *wat*, which refers to a temple/monastery complex comprising several distinct religious buildings, in addition to monks' residential quarters.

The principal structure is the *bot*, the most sacred part of the temple and the place where ordination ceremonies are conducted. The building is identified by eight boundary stones, called *sima*, placed outside at the four corners and the four cardinal points. A temple is also likely to have one or more *viharn*, a building used as a sermon hall for monks and lay worshippers.

Architecturally, the *bot* and *viharn* are virtually identical, being rectangular buildings with sweeping roofs covered with glazed tiles. Each end of the roof's peak terminates in a gilded finial known as a *cho fa*, or 'sky tassel'. A gracefully curved ornamentation, it looks like a slender bird's neck and head, and is generally believed to represent the mythical Garuda, half bird, half man.

Another characteristic of temple structures is the *chedi* or *stupa*. Dominating the compound of a *wat*, this is a tall decorative spire constructed over relics of the Buddha, sacred texts or an image. Essentially there are two basic forms: bell-shaped and raised on square or round terraces of diminishing size, and tapering to a thin spire; or a round, finger-like tower. The latter, derived from Khmer architecture and symbolic of the mythical mountain abode of the gods, is known as a *prang*.

Other buildings in a temple compound can include a library for sacred texts, and a *mondop*, a square-shaped building with tapering roof enshrining some relic, often a Buddha footprint, a stone impression far larger than life-size. Some larger *wats* may also have cloisters, open-sided galleries perhaps displaying rows of Buddha images, while bell towers and pavilions can be additional features. *Wats* further have a crematorium, identified by its needle-like chimney and, usually, a school for monks and perhaps also for lay children.

Rather like a medieval Christian church, the Thai temple was the focal point of every village. Unlike the church, however, it served far more than the community's spiritual needs. In the past, and still today in some rural areas, cultural life revolved around the *wat* which stood as social services centre, school, hospital, dispensary, hostelry, and village news, employment and information agency.

The earliest Thai temple buildings were strongly influenced by Khmer architecture with, for example, sandstone being used for door posts, lintels and rectangular windows. Later, from around the 12th century, brick replaced sandstone, the surface being finished with a stucco covering. But more characteristic than the materials is the ornamental decoration of Thai temples.

Probably initially derived from Chinese examples, Thai temple ornamentation is profuse, polychromatic and richly detailed. Roofs are tiled in orange and green, gables and spires are gilded, coloured glass mosaic adorns pediments and pillars. No surface is left unadorned and a remarkable array of techniques and materials are brought into play – woodcarving, stucco relief, lacquer, gilt, mother-of-pearl inlay, gold leaf and porcelain fragments. It all sounds far too much, but surprisingly such a seeming excess of ornamentation succeeds and the greatest achievement of the most traditional form of Thai architecture has been the decorative, not the monumental.

Domestic architecture is less obviously derivative of other cultures and less flamboyant than the temple. The traditional teakwood house tries to blend typical Thai characteristics of grace and pragmatism.

A vital distinction of Thai-style houses is that they were intended to be portable. In the past when people moved house, they did literally that. Posts and panels would be carted off and re-assembled at a new site, a task that could be accomplished in a single day with the help of neighbours.

As prefabricated structures, Thai houses have walls of movable panels, frequently made in standard sizes so as to be interchangeable. These are assembled on site and are attached to a superstructure of sturdy columns and beams. Holding everything together are wooden pegs, non-wooden elements being rare in traditional Thai houses.

Roofs, covered with either wooden or ceramic tiles, are steeply sloped and given

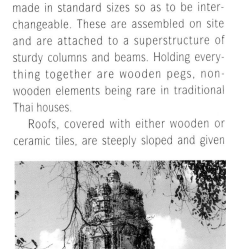

The bell-shaped chedi's *supremely elegant proportions are exemplified by Sukhothai's Wat Sra Sri* (above); *the* prang, *a different type of* chedi, *found full expression at Ayutthaya* (above, far right).

Sweeping temple roofs are most often tiled in orange and green, as at Bangkok's Wat Arun (above, centre). *'Sky tassels',* cho fa, *top all gable peaks while bargeboards, as at Wat Phra That Haripunchai, Lamphun* (right), *are intricately carved and decorated.*

a broad overhang to provide protection from the bright sunlight and the monsoon rains. There may also be a second, stepped roof level to facilitate ventilation.

Frequently located by a river or canal, the entire house is raised a couple of metres off the ground on sturdy pillars so as to give protection from floods and from snakes and other wild animals, as well as to allow air circulation. In former times, the ground floor space also provided sleeping quarters for the family's livestock.

Completing the basic design is a verandah. This is an integral element in a dwelling where almost half the space is set aside for outdoor living, and apart from affording a shady spot for escaping the worst heat of the day, the verandah can be turned into a kitchen garden with potted plants, a welcome convenience in times of floods.

Thai-style houses may be simple or complex. The essential unit is a rectangle some 3.5 by 9 metres (11 x 30 feet), the interior providing one or two rooms, but the living area can be easily enlarged with the addition of further units. As many as eight or ten components, arranged around an open central platform, can be integrated to produce one large dwelling sufficient to accommodate the extended family.

Besides the temple and the teakwood house, the only other local architecture of note is the shophouse, or *hong thaew* (literally 'room row'), which was the most ubiquitous secular building during the early years of modern commercial development. A shophouse, or rowshop, is precisely what the name implies, one of a row of shops with a simple but supremely functional design. Each unit is basically an oblong box, one room wide and three or four storeys high. The ground floor is used for commercial purposes – a shop, a restaurant, a workshop, warehouse or whatever – while the upper floors provide living quarters for the owner of the business and his family. Making its first appearance in Bangkok around the middle of the 19th century, the shophouse was the standard structure for building expansion in virtually every city and town in the country, until very recently.

Today, in the wake of rapid economic development, Bangkok and, to a lesser degree other big cities, display the now familiar pattern of post-modern international architecture — high-rises with glass curtain walls, office towers, condominiums, luxury hotels, shopping malls and housing estates. Bangkok in particular presents a fruit salad of architectural styles, from Classical Greek to Post Modern. House designs may range from a Roman villa to mock-Tudor, or a condominium can be bizarrely modelled on a Gothic cathedral.

SCULPTURE

Virtually all classical Thai fine art is religious art, produced in the service of Buddhism, and sculpture is primarily the art of fashioning Buddha images in a profusion and beauty of form that are unmatched. More than any other type of art work, Buddha sculptures exemplify the Kingdom's aesthetic achievement and link 13 centuries of tradition which have moulded the artistic development of the land.

In this there is a curious irony. While Thai Buddha statues display high aesthetic standards and meticulous workmanship, the image has never been conceived nor perceived as a work of art. In their commissioning and fashioning, images were viewed as objects of devotion whose creation was an act of merit-making, not of self-expression.

There have been many shifting emphases in influence and style but, at the same time, artists were kept to strict guidelines and had to reproduce certain features and attitudes that were traditional and accepted as integral. Accordingly all images possess certain common features.

Firstly, the Buddha, as the Great Teacher, is represented as a human being,

Traditional Thai houses were designed for portability; many fine examples from different regions are now located in Bangkok. The classic teak Kamthieng House (above), *set in the grounds of the Siam Society, is from the North; from near Ayutthaya and other areas came the delightful pavilions* (left), *now preserved in the garden of the Suan Pakkard Palace .*

and yet the Enlightened One is understood as a remarkable personage, bearing 32 major and 80 minor marks which distinguished him from other mortals. Characteristic are the *ushnisha* or cranial protuberance, hair curling in a clockwise direction, extended ear lobes, flat feet and projecting heels. In form, images were confined to just four postures – walking, standing, seated and reclining – while the positions of the hands were fixed in any one of a number of established *mudras* or gestures signifying certain attitudes, such as meditation, teaching and dispelling fear.

The earliest Buddha images discovered in the land now encompassed by Thai national borders are examples of Indian sculpture from the Gupta (4th–6th centuries) and Pala (8th–11th centuries) schools. The first style produced locally, although belonging to a pre-Thai civilization, is that of Dvaravati.

At best in stone and terracotta, Dvaravati art is fundamentally Theravada Buddhist and in its early phases was heavily influenced by India. From the middle phase (8th or 9th century) Indian models were followed less slavishly and Dvaravati images become distinct in being less massive, more simplified and with gradually more indigenous physical characteristics such as a flatter face, broader nose and thicker lips.

While Dvaravati held sway over central Thailand, the south was under another powerful kingdom, that of Srivijaya which dominated the Malay Peninsula from the 8th century to about the end of the 13th. Srivijaya images differ from those of Dvaravati in that they reflected the Mahayana rather than Theravada sect of Buddhism. Thus Bodhisattvas were widely portrayed, an outstanding example being a statue of Avalokitesvara discovered in Chaiya. Dating from the 8th or 9th century, the figure is remarkable for its serene and tranquil expression and is a brilliant work of art judged by any standards. Also notable among the later Srivijaya period are images of the Buddha seated beneath a *naga* (mythical snake).

Khmer, or Lopburi art, as it is also known, is dated as lasting from the 11th to the 14th centuries. Lopburi Buddha images were both carved in stone and cast in bronze, and typical characteristics are the

Classical Thai sculpture has been devoted principally to the making of images of the Buddha; the different schools of art that sprang up over the centuries exhibited varying stylistic features. Sukhothai Buddhas (above left) are highly regarded for their serene and slender grace; Lopburi images (above right) show strong Khmer influences while early Chiang Saen examples (right) are more reminiscent of Indian Buddhist sculpture.

cranial protuberance modified into three rows of lotus petals and a lotus bud halo.

It was at the first Thai capital, Sukhothai, that Thai art had its finest flowering and arguably the most beautiful and most truly original Buddha images date from this period. Dated between the late 13th and early 15th centuries, Sukhothai images were far more stylized than anything that had gone before and are marked by a greater fluidity in the line of the body and an uncanny degree of serenity and spirituality expressed in the facial features.

Statues in the seated posture were popular but the real triumph of the Sukhothai artists, and perhaps the highest aesthetic achievement of all Thai sculpture, was the walking Buddha. This posture had appeared before but only in carved relief and it was a

Thai innovation to produce walking images in the round. Not only was originality achieved, it was achieved in a most stunning fashion with the artists brilliantly capturing their subject in a frozen moment of movement with one heel raised and the other foot firmly planted on the ground; one arm swings freely at the side while the other expresses a *mudra*.

At roughly the same time as Sukhothai was consolidating its nation status, the Thais in the north of the country were united in the Lanna kingdom which had its capital at Chiang Mai, founded in 1296. Its school of art is generally referred to as Chiang Saen style, named after the town which was an early power centre of the region and where a number of images of great merit have been found.

The fine temple murals at Wat Phumin, Nan, which show scenes from the Jataka *tales, provide numerous fascinating, and often humorous, glimpses of the daily life and society of a hundred years ago.*

Chiang Saen art is commonly dated between the 11th and 18th centuries, and falls into two broad groups, early and late. Distinctive characteristics of early Chiang Saen Buddhas are a halo in the form of a lotus bud, round face, prominent chin and stout body with a well developed chest. The later period, at its height during the reign of King Tilokaraja (1442–87), coincides with the blossoming of Theravada Buddhism in the north and shows both Sukhothai and Sri Lankan influences in the flame-shaped halo, oval face and more slender body of the Buddha images.

The sculpture of the Ayutthaya period is divided into two categories, that of U-Thong or early Ayutthaya (*c*.12th–15th centuries) and Ayutthaya proper which spans the period from the mid 14th to mid 18th centuries. U-Thong images are essentially typified by a square face and a stern expression. Even those most strongly marked by the impact of Sukhothai models are less stylized than the originals and show a more human anatomy. In the Ayutthaya style proper the heritage of Sukhothai came to outweigh that of the Khmer but the U-Thong form never completely vanished and the Buddha images of this period are scarcely comparable to the achievements of Sukhothai's Golden Age.

The current period of Thai art, that of Bangkok (or Rattanakosin), dates from the establishment of that city as the capital in 1782. During the first reign of the present Chakri dynasty few new Buddha images were produced and temples were decorated with statues that were collected from around the country.

In the reigns of King Rama II (1809–24) and King Rama III (1824–51) crowned Buddhas were produced but, as with those of Ayutthaya, more emphasis was given to the decoration than to the facial expression. Yet one masterpiece does date from the reign of King Rama III and that is the giant statue of the reclining Buddha enshrined at Wat Po. Its massive size tends to overpower more aesthetic considerations but it is none the less an extremely serene image.

Increasingly in the Bangkok period artists have tended to produce more lifelike images and while certain traditional characteristics are shown, the overall effect is that of a more humanized figure. A fine example is the standing Buddha made in 1957 to commemorate the 2,500th anniversary of Buddhism and today housed at the Phuttha Monthon (Buddha Mandala) at Nakhon Pathom, west of Bangkok.

If the context in which Buddha images were produced was anonymous and bound by convention, enormous freedom existed in the choice of medium available to sculptors. Images have been fashioned in virtually every suitable material – wood, terracotta, stone, stucco, crystal, ivory, silver, gold, jasper and other semi-precious stones. Brick and mortar was widely used for monumental statues. But above all bronze has long been the favoured medium for Thai Buddha images, and has also made a not inconsiderable contribution to the intrinsic distinction of the Thai style.

PAINTING

Painting in the Western sense of individual artists expressing their own visions on canvas or other surfaces did not exist in Thailand until the 20th century. Prior to that visual art was religious in concept and content, and limited almost exclusively to temple murals and, to a lesser extent, illustrated manuscripts.

Individual in form and accomplished in technique, temple mural paintings are in many respects the most fascinating of all Thailand's classical arts. Regrettably, fine early examples are rare. Fragile due to the techniques used and perishable in the surfaces employed, they have suffered the ravages of time and climate. So much has already been lost that the art form is best known today by murals dating from the fall of Ayutthaya in 1767 to around 1910 when traditional painting went into decline.

While no examples survive, there is sufficient evidence to suggest that painting was a developed art in Thailand as early as the Dvaravati period (7th–11th centuries). The earliest styles would most likely have been subject to strong Indian influences, but the later impact of the Singhalese school and its modification during the Sukhothai era (late 13th–early 15th centuries) led to the beginnings of an indigenous Buddhist graphic art. By the 18th century mural painting had achieved a popularity such that the work then being executed can be considered as an art form unique to Thailand.

All Thai mural paintings are primarily didactic in purpose, aiming to instruct the people in Buddhist principles commonly by depicting scenes from the Buddha's life and his previous incarnations. As religious art, murals were moreover executed essentially as offerings and in that sense contain no conscious individual expression; with only a few exceptions the artists remained anony-

Scenes from the Ramakien, *the Thai version of the Indian epic tale the* Ramayana, *are depicted in the Inner Cloister murals, painted between 1825 and 1850, at Wat Phra Keo, Bangkok.*

mous. However, there was usually sufficient scope for the artistic sense not to be stifled. Decorative and poetic qualities are of a high order in the best works.

The mural adornment of a *bot*, where the temple's most sacred Buddha image is enshrined, follows a set pattern. The two side walls are decorated with scenes from the life of the Buddha, the *Jataka* tales (past lives) and sometimes registers of heavenly beings kneeling in postures of devotion. The wall behind the presiding Buddha statue is generally covered with a diagrammatic interpretation of the Buddhist cosmology, and the facing wall usually has a scene of the victory over *Mara*, an allegory of the triumph over the temptation of evil.

As the convention was to fill the entire painted area, backgrounds were often completed with genre scenes and views of daily life, commonly expressed with a marked sense of humour. Here the artists had scope for individual expression, and these mural details are frequently extremely accomplished, fascinating for their glimpses of ordinary society.

Hand-made blue-and-white pottery, in both typical (above) *and contemporary patterns, is a thriving industry and successful export.*

CONTEMPORARY ART

Thai art has come a long way in the 20th century. Throwing off the shackles of repetitive temple mural painting in the early decades of the 1900s, art in Thailand has opened itself up to the quest for a new aesthetic, not hidebound by parochial traditions yet still true to cultural roots.

Modern art essentially dates from 1933 when Italian sculptor Corrado Feroci (who later adopted the Thai name Silpa Bhirasri) was employed by the government to establish a school of Fine Arts in Bangkok which, a decade later, became Silpakorn University. Feroci formalized a curriculum based on the Western pattern, and for the first time art students could follow an academic course instead of the old master-pupil apprenticeship under which all artists had previously learnt their craft.

Since the 1930s, painters have sought, with uneven results, to find a Thai mode of expression speaking an international language. After working their way through the Western 'isms', from Impressionism to Postmodernism via Cubism and Surrealism, the best artists are now beginning to create more original, vital works with indigenous content. Cultural assumptions, however, continue to inhibit development.

The context in which art is now being produced is, however, extremely vibrant. Bangkok's art scene booms and prices soar. There are more galleries in the capital now than at any other time, and more exhibitions are being held in an ever-greater diversity of venues from the National Gallery to smart hotel lobbies.

At the moment, Thailand's leading artists are commanding unprecedented prices. Thawan Duchanee, for example, can earn upwards of US$12,000 a picture. Displaying draughtsmanship of genius, Thawan's most typical works are convoluted intensely detailed drawings, frequently depictions of either muscle-bound human forms or haunting and sometimes frightening phantasmagoric animals. Perhaps the most original element in Thawan's work is its masculine quality, its sense of strength and power. This is something quite new for Thai art, which traditionally has been soft and decorative.

Holding the limelight with Thawan is Pratuang Emcharoen, a self-taught artist and one-time poster painter. He tends towards prismatic colours and a cosmic style while drawing inspiration for his work from Nature and natural forms.

While the religious murals of the past still exert an influence and some fine contemporary painters continue to explore inner spiritual life, more artists are beginning to look to their immediate surroundings for inspiration, taking everyday objects for their materials and social issues for their themes. In simplified terms, the best younger artists work in one of two main streams, neo-traditionalism and contemporary. A good example of the first is Panya Vijinthanasarn whose works give modern expression to classical mural motifs. In the contemporary field, Montien Boonma is achieving recognition as a conceptual artist employing Western techniques in mixed-media installations which possess an essentially new and Thai content.

POTTERY

Throughout the history of Thai pottery there has been a remarkably consistency of aesthetic accomplishment, while forms have evolved with enormous stylistic variation. Even common or garden wares, such as 'klong jars' and 'dragon jars' (large water containers with a dragon decorative motif) possess artistic merit.

Excavations during the late 1960s and early 1970s at Ban Chiang in north-east Thailand revealed evidence of an agrarian,

The classical dance drama khon *re-enacts the legendary story of the* Ramakien. *Elaborately decorated brocade costumes are worn by all performers and stylized* khon *masks by those playing giants or animals.*

bronze-making culture dating back to 3600 BC For historians this triggered much perplexed re-thinking about the cradles of civilization, but the most exciting finds in artistic terms were beautiful pieces of unglazed red-on-buff hand-painted pottery.

Found in various forms – pots, vases, jars, figurines and other items – Ban Chiang pottery displays an enormous variety of skilled and aesthetically pleasing shapes. It is even more distinguished by its decorative designs of, typically, whorls and loops in which high artistic achievement lies behind deceptively simple patterns.

Moving into the period of recorded history, the first notable pottery is that of the Mon kingdom of Dvaravati. The Mon were skilled in the production of both earthenware and terracotta, and the art survives today among the Mon community at Kao Kred island in the Chao Phraya river, a little way upstream from Bangkok, where a low-fired, unglazed earthenware known as *Pim Lai* is produced.

The Thais were no less skilled in pottery than their predecessors. During the Sukhothai era, Thai ceramics enjoyed a golden age. Production occurred at various centres but most especially at Si Satchanalai, near Sawankhalok, the latter name being given to the distinctive wares of the period. Output was enormous, consisting of a huge range of everyday and decorative items, from pots, bowls and plates to figurines, and production was for export as well as domestic consumption.

As varied as the range of objects produced during the Sukhothai period are the types of pottery. Earthenware, stoneware, unglazed, underglazed black decorated wares and more were all part of the output, but the most famous is celadon. Possibly meaning 'sheathed in jade', celadon is a term applied to a distinctive group of high-fired stoneware, covered with a natural feldspathic, wood-ash glaze containing iron, and fired in a reduction atmosphere. Jade green is the popular colour, although hues range from near-white through sea-blue/green to brown.

Important among other wares found in Thailand are the Sino-Thai ceramics of *bencharong, lai nam thong* and blue-and-white porcelain. None of these was originally an indigenous craft, all being Chinese export items specifically designed for the Thai market, but they are today locally produced. Antique and contemporary wares, therefore, are to be found.

Bencharong (the name translates as 'five colours') is a porcelain decorated with highly ornate and intricate patterns in a multi-coloured enamel. *Lai nam thong* is similar though with a greater emphasis on gold enamel. Although originally made in China, the designs of these wares are strikingly and unmistakably Thai.

Commonly in the form of lidded bowls, dishes, cups and spoons, frequently made in sets, the best quality *bencharong* was once usually reserved for royal and ceremonial use. The craft peaked in the first part of the current Rattanakosin period and then declined in the later 19th century with the arrival of mass-produced porcelain from abroad. In recent years production has been renewed and modern wares are readily available. Antique pieces are rare and highly priced.

Blue-and-white wares, again in a variety of forms, are clearly Chinese in decorative style. Early pieces in Thailand date back to 15th–17th century Ayutthaya, while modern hand-made blue-and-white is a thriving local industry, notably in the northern town of Lampang.

Thai pottery today is a booming industry reproducing excellent quality wares in virtually all the major styles of the past. Yet it would be wrong to think that the craft is now devoid of creativity and innovation. The present-day ceramics industry is vibrant, both in the re-interpretation of the traditional and in contemporary designs.

THE PERFORMING ARTS

Thailand has a long tradition of performing arts, with both dance and puppetry dating from Ayutthaya times. The two are closely allied in terms of narrative content and style, although puppetry, performed with different types of marionettes operated from above by strings or from below by rods (cut-out hide shadow puppets are also traditional to southern Thailand), is all but extinct today. Dance, on the other hand, has survived, albeit precariously

The two major forms of Thai classical dance drama are *khon* and *lakon nai*. Both were originally exclusively court entertainments, and it was not until much later that a popular style of dance theatre, *likay*, evolved as a diversion for the common folk who had no access to court performances.

Khon is a masked dance dramatization of the *Ramakien*, the Thai version of the Indian moral epic the *Ramayana*. Developing out of shadow-play in the 16th century, a full performance demands a vast cast of actors playing the roles of gods, giants, men, monkey warriors and assorted beasts. All the characters were at one time depicted by the actors wearing elaborate masks, but in latter-day shows only the masks of giants and animals have been retained. Nevertheless, any narrative is still left to a chorus, and actors keep their faces expressionless, communicating solely through a complex vocabulary of hand gestures and body movements.

Lakon nai may take its narrative content from a variety of legends, the *Inaw*, another princely tale, being one of the most popular. Masks are not worn by the dancers.

Traditionally, *lakon nai* was danced exclusively by women and *khon* only by men. Such a division between the sexes is no longer strictly adhered to, but it does point to a more vital distinction between the two dramatic styles. While both rely on gesture and posture as modes of expressing emotion as well as action, the *khon* actor seeks virtuosity in strength and agility and muscular exertion, the *lakon nai* dancer is persuasive through grace and remarkably controlled movement.

Serving as a counterpoint to the control and restraint of the dance itself are the costumes which are extremely rich and flamboyant. Made of intricately embroidered cloth, a leading male attire comprises a tight-fitting jacket, breeches and a loin cloth worn outside and held in place by a broad sash and a bejewelled belt. Ornaments such as bracelets, armlets and rings add further to a picture of sartorial splendour. For female players the typical dress is a long skirt and cape, pointed golden headdress and other jewellery that rivals if not surpasses the glory of the male.

Dancers do not wear make-up as in the Western theatrical tradition, where it is used to alter appearance to a greater or lesser extent, and instead facial features are merely accentuated in the usual manner. The *khon* masks are similarly conventional in the way that they depend on colour symbolism and stylized design to depict the various characters, rather than make any attempt to portray the life-like.

Music is integral to all forms of Thai dance drama and performances are accompanied by an orchestra comprising traditional instruments, usually five percussion pieces and one woodwind. Small bell-like cymbals are used to set the pace while the music of the rest of the orchestra lends mood. Like most other aspects of classical

Sinuous, graceful movements and gestures, especially of the arms and hands, characterize the lakon nai *form of classical dance drama.*

Thai theatre, the orchestra is bound by convention. Essentially the tunes are indicative of specific actions and emotions, so there are 'walking tunes', 'marching tunes', 'laughing tunes', 'weeping tunes', 'anger tunes' and so on. Such passages are instantly recognizable by an audience accustomed to Thai musical notation and composition.

If *khon* and *lakon nai* can be compared as art to western ballet, *likay* is the equivalent of pantomime. The dramatic content is standard, full of the tried and tested stuff of melodrama – crossed lovers, maidens in distress, lost princes finally reunited with their patrimony, and so forth. Improvisation, however, plays an important part, and one performance can differ markedly from another depending on the actors' quick wits and fertile sense of humour. Puns, verbal virtuosity and slapstick humour are *likay*'s stock-in-trade.

Costumes are allowed to run riot and there is a tendency for gaudy jewellery, grossly accentuated make-up, bright colours and generally raffish dress. Together it amounts to, as one commentator has remarked, 'imaginative bad taste'.

LITERATURE

Thailand's literary tradition consists largely of mythological and historical fables. The majority of these are of Indian origin, but they have been so extensively revised and rewritten to suit local tastes and ideas as to become to all intents and purposes uniquely Thai in style and content.

The most famous tale of all, and one which has had an all-pervading influence on Thai classical arts, is the *Ramakien*, the Thai version of the Indian allegorical epic, the *Ramayana*. A moral tale concerning the struggles of Prince Rama and Hanuman's monkey army against the forces of evil, the saga opens with the founding of the rival cities of Ayutthaya, capital of the gods, and Langka, city of the demons. In what is a long and convoluted narrative, the principal action is episodic and focuses on the trials and tribulations of Ayutthaya's Prince Rama, the abduction of his wife, Sita, and the eventual defeat of Langka by Hanuman and his army of monkey warriors.

Reputedly written some 2,000 years ago and accredited to the Indian poet Valmiki, the *Ramakien* was early on incorporated, in one form or another, into the cultures of almost all South-east Asian civilizations, and was firmly established before the rise of the Thai kingdom. But early Thai versions were lost during the sack of Ayutthaya by the Burmese in 1767, and the fullest of the existing texts was written in 1807 by King Rama I, assisted by court poets.

Further royal patronage of the Thai literary tradition includes two episodes of the *Ramakien* which King Rama II composed for classical dance drama, the most common medium, along with the visual arts, in which the epic found expression. Other literary compositions by King Rama II include several epic poems – the best known being the *Inaw*, a romance with a Javanese background, although full of details illustrating Thai customs, habits and manners, as well as historical information. The monarch also collaborated with court poets, the finest of whom was Sunthorn Phu (1786–1855), widely regarded as Thailand's greatest literary figure. His highest achievement was to write supremely well in ordinary language, rather than in the courtly style, and thus appeal to all classes. His best known work, which has become a Thai classic, is *Phra Aphai Mani*, a romantic adventure concerning the odyssey of an exiled prince.

Popular literature throughout Thai history has had an oral rather than a written tradition, with well-known and well-loved tales transmitted by village storytellers. Legends, anecdotes and adventure yarns abound, although perhaps the most popular tales to survive are those concerning a peasant-born trickster known as Sri Thanonchai, whose numerous, often bizarre and hilarious escapades are played out largely against the background of medieval court life. The stories' timeless appeal, however, springs from Sri Thanonchai's endearing combination of cunning insolence and acute native wit which he employs to full effect in constant brushes with officialdom. As in many popular tales, humour, often earthy and bawdy, is a common element.

In the field of non-fiction, palm-leaf and paper manuscripts were widely produced. Because of the fragile medium, however, few surviving examples predate the 18th century. Written on long concertina-folded pages and often accompanied by beautifully painted illustrations, manuscripts covered the whole gamut of knowledge from religious texts to treatises on such diverse

Many examples of traditional Thai craftsmanship can be seen at Wat Phra Keo, Bangkok. Here, mythological demons, known as yaksha, *guard a golden* chedi.

subjects as elephant care, herbal medicine and military strategy.

Today, modern literature remains robust, particularly poetry which has always been a major art form; the Thais have an acute ear and great love for puns, play on words and verbal dexterity in general. There is also a considerable output of short stories and novels. Best known among the modern classics are probably the novels of the late elder statesman and former prime minister M.R. Kukrit Pramoj, whose major work, *Si Phandin* ('Four Reigns'), is set against the background of courtly life during the reigns of Kings Rama V to Rama VIII.

CRAFTS

The Thais are adept at numerous crafts, their techniques handed down from generation to generation. Some, like silk and cotton weaving, have been long-held occupations of country folk, with production initially for domestic use until the later creation of commercial markets.

Most visible of the local craft traditions are the decorative arts, for which the Thais

possess a true genius. These range from the woodcarving and coloured glass mosaic used in the external decoration of temples, to black lacquer-and-gilt inlay work and mother-of-pearl inlay, both employed in furniture (manuscript cabinets, for example), doors and other flat surfaces.

Among handicrafts, the most famous today is hand-woven Thai silk. Produced in countless colours and designs, Thai silk was customarily used for clothing, but with the advent of mass-produced dress, the craft was in danger of dying out until it was revived in the 1950s as a commercial product, largely due to the efforts of the American entrepreneur, Jim Thompson. One of the best places for visitors to buy high-quality silks is at the Silk Company shop in Bangkok, near Thompson's beautiful teak house, now a museum. Today, Thai silk is woven in heavier weights ideal for draperies, upholstery and other household furnishing, while the rich fabric is further used for place mats and napkins, scarves and other accessories.

The most highly-prized of the traditional silks is a form known as *mat mee*, a fabric unique to north-east Thailand. Produced from tie-dyed silk threads, the fabric is hand-woven in a variety of beautiful designs, typically distinguished by intricate patterns and subtle colours. Once a neglected craft, *mat mee* silk has been revitalized in recent years through rural development projects initiated by Her Majesty Queen Sirikit. Today, the fabric enjoys an unprecedented vogue as a fashion material favoured by Her Majesty and other members of the Royal Family.

Of note among a host of other handicrafts — beaten silverware, lacquerware, basketry, paper umbrellas, rattan and wicker furniture — is nielloware. Practised in southern Thailand for hundreds of years, this is the craft of decorating gold and silver objects with delicate etched designs filled with a metal alloy. Workmanship of high quality is found in various objects, such as trays, boxes and vases.

THAILAND NORTH TO SOUTH

THE NORTH

Chiang Rai Thailand's northernmost province, Chiang Rai is an area of high forested hills and fertile valleys. It is bordered by Myanmar (Burma) to the west and north, and by Laos to the north-west, the latter boundary formed by the Mekong river. There are two notable tributaries: the Kok river, which flows through Chiang Rai town, and the tiny Ruak whose confluence with the Mekong joins the borders of Thailand, Myanmar and Laos, forming the so-called 'Golden Triangle', now groomed as a tourist spot.

With an economy still largely based on agriculture, the region retains a typically Thai rural character and is notable for its unspoilt scenery. An exotic element is provided by the presence of six distinct tribal minorities — Yao, Akha, Lahu, Hmong, Lisu and Karen — who cling to independent lifestyles in spite of the encroachment of mainstream society. Some, but by no means all, of the hilltribes continue to cultivate the opium poppy, and the drug trade adds a spurious reputation to the 'Golden Triangle'.

The main town and provincial capital, Chiang Rai, was briefly in the mid-13th century capital of a small fiefdom, but was soon surpassed by Chiang Mai to the south. Today, it retains a tranquil, traditional air, although it is poised to become the hub of a trade zone comprising neighbouring areas of Myanmar, Laos and China's Yunnan Province —what the phrase-makers term the 'Golden Quadrangle'. Sights in the town include a handful of venerable temples, the most famous of which is Wat Phra Keo where the Emerald Buddha image, now in Bangkok, was first discovered.

Chiang Mai Located directly south-east of Chiang Rai, Chiang Mai is the North's largest province. It is similarly an area of high hills (including Thailand's highest peak, Doi Inthanon, now a national park) cut through north to south by rivers, the most important being the Ping. The valleys, however, are broader, a topographical advantage which led to Chiang Mai city being

Many regional Thai crafts have enjoyed a revival under the patronage of Her Majesty the Queen. Today, handicrafts flourish throughout the country. For the visitor, the variety can be overwhelming: gaily decorated umbrellas from the North (above left), intricate yan lipao *basketry from the South (above right), exquisite hand-woven silks (right), and stylish silverware (below right) are among the many goods on offer.*

Wood carvers are some of Thailand's most skilled craftsmen, turning their talents today, as in the past, to both temple decoration and domestic pieces. Among the finest early examples of the craft are the famous carved doors at Wat Phumin, Nan (far right).

Throughout Thailand, traditional and modern forms of transport co-exist. The horse-drawn carriages of Lampang (above right) allow for a relaxed pace, as do samlors, the pedal-powered bicycle rickshaws found all over the country (opposite, bottom left). Far less sedate, *and certainly noisier, are the motorized* tuk-tuk *rickshaws (above left and opposite, right) that buzz about towns and cities, and the unique 'longtail' boats (opposite, top left) that ply many waterways and coastal regions.*

founded in 1296 as the capital of Lanna, a Thai kingdom which supplanted the off-shoot Mon principality of Haripunchai (present-day Lamphun, now capital of its own tiny province).

Chiang Mai is Thailand's second city (in area, not population, which is little more than 150,000) and the unofficial capital of the North. Once a charming backwater, renowned for its temples and wealth of traditional handicrafts, the city is today experiencing the stresses and strains of rapid modern development. None the less, like the rest of the North, it retains much of the distinct character that arose from its separate history, most notable in dialect, cuisine, festivals and a greater adherence to traditional values. In spite of Chiang Mai's recent growth, agriculture is still an important economic activity, and the region, with cooler temperatures in the hills, is noted in particular for its fruit and flowers more typical of temperate climes.

Mae Hong Son The North's westernmost province, Mae Hong Son, is a delightfully remote area bordering the Shan hills of Myanmar (Burma). With hidden valleys, any

one a contender for Shangri-La, it possesses arguably the most picturesque scenery. Until the mid 1960s, when a highway from Chiang Mai was first opened, the provincial capital, Mae Hong Son, was effectively cut off from the rest of the country. Although modern development is slowly catching up with the town, nature still dominates and the impression is one of tranquillity.

Culturally as well as geographically Mae Hong Son is a little island cut off from the rest of Thailand. A distinct character is preserved not only by old wooden houses and ageing Burmese-style temples, but also by the people, the majority of whom are Thai Yai or Shan, while Karen, Meo, Lisu and Lahu inhabit the surrounding hills.

Lampang Due east of Chiang Mai, Lampang is an important province, its capital of the same name being a major junction on the principal north-south highway. Located on the banks of the Wang river, the town has a long history and has been inhabited since the 7th century, when it was a part of the Mon kingdom of Haripunchai. In the early 20th century, Lampang was a centre of the teak trade and while those days

have now passed, it remains a significant commercial hub. Like the North's other eastern provinces, Lampang is more typically and traditionally Thai than Chiang Mai. Sights include several well-preserved temples that display Burmese influence in their architecture and decorative details.

Nan Beyond the provinces of Phrae and Phayao, both sites of early settlements but now largely backwaters and scenically undistinguished, is the North's easternmost province of Nan. Once the centre of a petty kingdom, conquered by Lanna in 1449, Nan was until the 1970s one of the country's most remote regions where bandits and communist insurgents hampered the building of roads and other infrastructure. Although development is now catching up with the place and Nan town is a bustling market town, the area remains off the beaten track and retains a rural air. Located on the banks of the Nan river, the provincial capital is, however, a fascinating town with a number of fine old temples, the most famous of which is Wat Phumin, while the province as a whole is one of

marked natural beauty, the hills bordering Laos being still densely forested.

Uttaradit The province's claim to fame is as the birthplace of King Taksin, the monarch who reunited the kingdom after the sack of Ayutthaya in 1767. Otherwise Uttaradit is notable only for its langsat fruit and the Sirikit Dam, Thailand's largest earth-filled dam.

THE CENTRE

Sukhothai Along with neighbouring Phitsanulok and Kamphaeng Phet provinces, Sukhothai was the cradle of the Thai nation. Here, in a landscape of low wooded hills, the first capital was founded in the mid-13th century. The ruins of Sukhothai, as well as those of its contemporary satellite towns, Si Satchanalai and Kamphaeng Phet, now preserved in manicured historical parks, rank among the most important ancient monuments in the country. Without notable ruins but boasting one superb temple, Phitsanulok, to the southeast, also has a long history as a strategic point between Sukhothai and Ayutthaya.

In marked contrast to past glories, modern towns in the area generally lack distinction, Sukhothai being singularly bereft of beauty. Natural scenery is at its best in Thung Salaeng Luang National Park, lying east of Phitsanulok town and spreading into neighbouring Phetchabun province. Once a base for communist guerrillas, the 1,262-square kilometre (487-square mile) park comprises a string of limestone hills, mixed deciduous forest and meadows, and harbours a number of interesting mammal species including Elephant, Yellow-throated Marten and Masked Palm Civet.

Tak Essentially a border province, Tak is both the gateway to the North (the provincial capital of the same name stands on the main north-south highway), while its western edge forms the frontier with Myanmar (Burma), delineated in part by the Moei river, newly bridged at the border town of Mae Sot. Traditionally considered a remote province, Tak is mostly forested and mountainous, and a somewhat sparse Thai population is supplemented by settlements of Hmong, Lahu, Lisu and Karen hilltribes.

Tak is slowly beginning to make a name for itself as an adventure travel destination, especially around the remote little town of Umphang, more an overgrown village, where the attraction of spectacular hill scenery is augmented by caves, waterfalls and facilities for river rafting.

Nakhon Sawan The sprawling provincial capital of Nakhon Sawan is a key market town and distribution centre in the upper part of the Central Plains. It does not boast any major sights, and although its character is coloured by a large proportion of its some 100,000 population being ethnic Chinese, it typifies in many ways the pattern that defines the central region. Nakhon Sawan draws strategic significance from its site at the junction of the Ping and Nan rivers, which merge to form the Chao Phraya, Thailand's principal waterway and lifeline of the Central Plains. This fertile and well-watered region is Thailand's heartland where traditionally most of the nation's rice is grown. The dozen or so generally small provinces which make up the Central Plains are characterized by a flat landscape

High-rise developments now line both its banks but Bangkok's 'River of Kings', the Chao Phraya, still retains its traditional role as a busy highway, transporting both goods and people along its waters.

of latter-day development, lie monuments to an extraordinarily rich past. Archaeological evidence suggests the area supported organized habitation in the prehistoric era and traces of a New Stone Age culture have been unearthed. Between the 7th and 11th centuries, Lopburi, then known as Louvo, was a major centre of the Dvaravati (Mon) Kingdom, the most influential cultural force in the Chao Phraya basin during the pre-Thai period. From the 10th to late 13th centuries the Khmer were dominant and Lopburi became an outpost of the Angkorian empire. Historical importance peaked in the 17th century when King Narai (1656–88) made Lopburi his second capital (after Ayutthaya), and it was here than many of the dramatic episodes of his eventful reign were played out. Substantial ruins survive from both the Khmer period and the 17th century to make the town rewarding in spite of its otherwise unpromising appearance.

divided into a patchwork of paddy fields interspersed with a number of sizeable towns and riverine settlements.

Uthai Thani Stretching to the western edge of the Central Plains and bordering the southern part of Tak, Uthai Thani is a marginal central province in that the flatlands give way to forest cover. Here Huai Kha Khaeng wildlife sanctuary stands as one of Thailand's best preserved natural habitats. Together with the neighbouring Thung Yai Naresuan sanctuary, it forms the heart of 15,000 square kilometres (5,792 square miles) of natural habitat containing examples of almost all the forest types of continental South-east Asia. It is home to a very diverse array of wildlife, including Elephant, Tiger and other wild cats, 50 per cent of the large birds and 33 per cent of the land vertebrates to be found in the region. The sanctuary is designated as a UN World Heritage Site and serves as a symbol for the rather fragile status of wildlife preservation generally in Thailand.

Ayutthaya Ayutthaya is both an exceptional province of the central region and in many ways the most typical. The flat, monotonous landscape is characteristic of the flood plains, which still support exten-

sive rice cultivation in spite of creeping urbanization and the construction of multilane highways. The town of Ayutthaya, however, is distinguished as the site of the nation's capital from the mid 14th century until 1767. Topographical reasons accounted for Ayutthaya's founding and its long-sustained prosperity. The fertile plains ensured a plentiful food supply, while the surrounding low-lying land, subject to seasonal flooding, afforded the city a degree of natural protection. Standing on the banks of the Chao Phraya river, at its junction with the Lopburi and Pa Sak rivers, Ayutthaya enjoyed the further advantage of an outlet to the sea, a vital factor in the age of waterborne commerce which coincided with Ayutthaya's rise. A network of canals, along with the riverine site, created an island city in which waterways provided the main transport and communication links.

Today, a dull provincial market town has grown up around the crumbling temples and other remains of what had been one of the largest and grandest cities in South-east Asia. None the less, the partially restored ruins give an inkling of past glories.

Lopburi Located north of Ayutthaya, Lopburi is superficially an undistinguished provincial centre. But hidden amid a maze

Suphan Buri Of the other central provinces lying north of Bangkok, Suphan Buri, west of Ayutthaya and Ang Thong, has a long history. The provincial capital of the same name dates back to the Dvaravati period, while later history is witnessed in a number of Ayutthaya-period temples. The present prosperous little town is characteristically central Thai.

Bangkok The present Thai capital, Bangkok was founded in 1782, prior to which it was little more than a trading post and front-line defence for Ayutthaya. The city proper stands on the east bank of the Chao Phraya river, some 40 kilometres (25 miles) from its mouth on the Gulf of Thailand, although Thonburi, on the west bank, is today included in the Greater Metropolitan area.

Like its predecessor, Ayutthaya, Bangkok was originally created as an island city by cutting a series of concentric canals which connected with the river — hence its old soubriquet 'Venice of the East'. Canals were the main means of transport and the first roads for wheeled traffic were not constructed until the mid 19th century.

In buildings as well as canals, Bangkok was initially modelled on Ayutthaya and was design to reflect the lost glory of that city. Later development, however, turned its back on the original heart with the result that Bangkok now sprawls monstrously over a flat alluvial plain. Accordingly there is no readily definable downtown area, just a cluster of districts distinct in character and with no obvious logical connection. The confusing appearance of the city is aggravated by notorious traffic congestion and increasingly appalling noise and air pollution.

None the less, Bangkok is the capital in every sense of the word. It is where the Royal Family resides, it is the seat of government and administration, and it is the focal point for virtually all major industrial, commercial and financial activity. It is also the country's main port, aviation gateway and home to well in excess of one-tenth of the country's total population.

Being all things, the city has borne the brunt of recent rapid and unprecedented economic growth. Increasing modernization has meant increasing Westernization and, accordingly, an apparent loss of identity. But Bangkok is essentially a paradox and while it embraces the new with enthusiasm, it also takes pride in the old. Thus gorgeous palaces and temples coexist with office towers, deluxe hotels and department stores.

Around Bangkok The several small provinces that surround Bangkok tend, like most satellite areas, to be overshadowed by the metropolis, although Samut Prakan, at the mouth of the Chao Phraya, Samut Sakorn and Samut Songkhram, noted for its salt flats, retain some of the traditional features of their coastal and estuary settings. Nakhon Pathom, due west of Bangkok, is, however, exceptional in its historical significance and its one major cultural site, the Phra Pathom Chedi, the world's tallest Buddhist monument at 120 metres (394 feet) high. Habitation of the area possibly dates back to the 3rd century BC, while the site of Nakhon Pathom town rose to prominence during the Dvaravati period (6th–11th centuries) as the likely capital of a Mon kingdom. It is widely believed to have been the earliest centre of Buddhist learning in the country.

Kanchanaburi West of Bangkok and abutting the mountains which divided Thailand from Myanmar (Burma), Kanchanaburi com-

bines historical interest with some of the most picturesque scenery in the whole country. The landscape is dominated by forested hills and the valleys of the Kwai Noi and Kwai Yai rivers which join at Kanchanaburi town to form the Mae Khlong river. Some of the most beautiful scenery is preserved at Erawan National Park, 550 square kilometres (212 square miles) of verdant hills with a seven-step stairway of waterfalls as its prime attraction. The park's mammal population includes Elephant, Banteng, Gaur, Sambar, Barking Deer and possibly Tiger and Leopard.

Historically Kanchanaburi is best known as the site of the Death Railway and Bridge over the River Kwai, built by allied POWs and Asian forced labour during World War II. The region, however, has a long past, with evidence of settlement during Neolithic times. In recorded history, the area was occupied by the ancient Khmer and, during the Thai period, was an invasion route, via the Three Pagodas Pass, for the Burmese.

Chachoengsao and Prachinburi The little-visited province of Chachoengsao, due east of Bangkok, traversed by the Bang Pakong river, presents a typical picture of provincial life, although it is famous for the

temple Wat Sothon Wararam Woravihara which enshrines the Phra Phuttha Sothon, one of the country's most sacred Buddha images found, according to legend, floating in the river.

Enveloping Chachoengsao to the north and east, is the boundary province of Prachinburi, bordering Cambodia. Thap Lan National Park, located in the vicinity of Na Di district, ranks as Thailand's second largest park at 2,240 square kilometres (865 square miles) and probably its least visited. The flora mostly belongs to the palm family, the Talipot Palm, or *lan* tree, giving the place its name.

THE EAST COAST

Chonburi Directly south-east of Bangkok, on the coast of the Gulf of Thailand, Chonburi was originally noted only for its agriculture, especially sugar cane and tapioca, and fishing. In recent decades, however, it has undergone enormous development. First, Pattaya, once a fishing village, was transformed into an international playground by the sea and is today grossly overbuilt, a victim of its own success. More recently, the Eastern Seaboard Development has transformed part of the coastline with the construction of deep-sea ports and industrial estates.

Within the massive crenellated walls that enclose Bangkok's Grand Palace and Wat Phra Keo, the nation's holiest shrine, gilded gables and soaring spires provide a scene of shimmering Oriental wonder.

Rayong, Chanthaburi and Trat These three provinces comprise the south-east corner of Thailand, the last two bordering Cambodia. The topography is defined by a narrow coastal plain backed by lush hills. Several beaches and offshore islands, notably Koh Samet, off the coast of Rayong, and Koh Chang (the country's second largest island at 492 square kilometres/190 square miles) in Trat, have been developed as seaside resorts. Away from the coast, fertile land in Trat and Chanthaburi yields a rich crop of fruit and vegetables, including durian, mangosteen and rambutan. Sapphires and rubies have also been extensively mined in the area, although the most productive gem fields are now mostly worked out.

Boats bob calmly in the setting sun off Pattaya, recalling this throbbing East Coast beach resort's early days as a quiet fishing village. Down the coast, Koh Chang still offers the simple beach life.

THE NORTH-EAST

Nakhon Ratchasima Commonly known as Khorat, Nakhon Ratchasima is Thailand's largest province, covering 20,500 square kilometres (7,915 square miles). The large provincial capital (population 205,000) is the region's gateway and typical of the several populous north-eastern cities which act as markets and service stations for the surrounding rural areas.

Before the scenery gives way to the semi-arid and mostly deforested plateau which comprises the North-east, Khao Yai National Park provides a topographical focal point. Spanning the bottom corner of Nakhon Ratchasima and spreading into neighbouring Saraburi, Nakhon Nayok and Prachinburi provinces, it covers 2,168 square kilometres (837 square miles) of forested hills and grassland, and is Thailand's oldest national park, founded in 1962. Natural beauty is matched by a wealth of wildlife, including some of the larger mammal species, notably, Elephant, Tiger, Leopard, Asiatic Black Bear, Malaysian Sun Bear, Barking Deer and Sambar Deer, while there are also over 300 species of birds and numerous butterflies.

Historically, the North-east was occupied by the ancient Khmer as witnessed by several superb temple ruins, among which 12th-century Phimai, which has been carefully restored, is the most famous.

Buriram Another of the North-east's largest and most populated provinces, Buriram borders Cambodia to the south

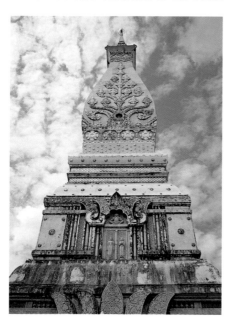

The Lao-style that of Wat That Phanom, the North-east's most sacred Buddhist shrine, dominates the temple complex.

and features several ancient Khmer temples, the biggest and best preserved being the hilltop Prasat Hin Khao Phanom Rung.

Khon Kaen and Roi Et Located in the heart of the North-east, Khon Kaen and Roi Et are mostly rural provinces where farming and hand-woven silk and other textiles are the principal occupations. Khon Kaen's provincial capital, however, is a large city and university town, the de facto capital of the North-east and focus of considerable modern development.

Udon Thani This is one of Thailand's fastest growing provinces. The provincial capital boomed initially when it was turned into a huge US air base during the Vietnam War, and the city has subsequently continued to prosper. But the province's major claim to fame is the prehistoric site of Ban Chiang where, in the 1970s, archaeological finds yielded evidence of early human habitation which set archaeologists rethinking the pattern of civilization. The finds, including skeletons, tools and distinctively patterned pottery have been dated as over 5,000 years old. Designated a World Heritage Site, Ban Chiang presents the earliest evidence of farming and the use of metals in the region.

Nong Khai Located on the banks of the Mekong river, opposite the Laotian capital of Vientiane, Nong Khai is an attractive province, fascinating for its river views. At Nong Khai town the Mekong is spanned by the 1190-metre (3,904-foot) Friendship Bridge, opened in 1994, and the charming little provincial capital, distinguished by a handful of temples, is becoming increasingly prosperous as a gateway to Laos.

Loei Although geographically located in the North-east, Loei has many features in common with the northern region. The landscape is one of high hills and mountains, and there is enormous climatic range, the province recording the country's highest and lowest temperatures — it is the only province where the mercury occasionally drops to 0°C (32°F). The provincial capital is small and unremarkable, while the rural life of the countryside remains essentially traditional. The major attractions are the national parks of Phu Kradung, Phu Luang and Phu Reua. All three are mountain areas with pines and abundant wildlife.

Nakhon Phanom Lying south-east of Nong Khai, Nakhon Phanom borders the Mekong and offers fine views across the river to the mountains of Laos. The province's principal sight is That Phanom, the most sacred shrine in the North-east. The site is possibly about 1,500 years old, although the present impressive 52-metre (170-foot) high *that* (Lao-style *chedi*) was rebuilt in 1978 after the previous structure collapsed during heavy rains. That Phanom is the venue for the region's biggest temple fair, celebrated on the full moon night of the third lunar month.

Sakon Nakhon The province is best known as the former home of two of Thailand's most revered Buddhist monks, Acharn Man, who died in 1949, and Acharn Fan who died in 1963. Both were believed to have attained exceptionally high levels of proficiency in the practice of meditation. Otherwise, Sakon Nakhon town has two important temples: Wat Phra That Choeng Chum, whose Lao-style *chedi* was built during the Ayutthaya period, and Wat Phra That Narai Cheng Weng which has a Khmer-period 12-metre (40-foot) high *prang*. On the eastern edge of town is Nong Han, Thailand's largest natural lake at 32 square kilometres (12 square miles).

Yasothon and Mukdahan Both these small provinces on the lower eastern side of the region are relatively new, Yasothon being created in 1972 and Mukdahan in 1982. They are mostly rural in character, although the latter draws distinction from its Mekong river frontage. Yasothon is famous for its annual Rocket Festival (*Bun*

Bang Fai), the region's largest traditional rain-invoking and fertility rite held in May. Huge homemade rockets are fired into the air to placate the sky god, while high-spirited revelry colours the two-day event.

Kalasin and Maha Sarakham In the centre of the North-east, these two neighbouring provinces are predominantly agricultural areas. Kalasin does have one or two interesting temples enshrining notable Buddha

A tranquil evening scene on the eastward-flowing Mun river near Ubon Ratchathani in the North-east. From here a scenic boat trip can be made to the Mun's confluence with the Mekong on the Thai/Lao border.

images. Particularly venerated by local worshippers is the Phra Buddha Saiyat Phu Khao, a reclining Buddha image dating from the late 17th century and different in that the figure lies on its left side instead of the more usual right.

Ubon Ratchathani The province ranks as the second largest in the North-east and its provincial capital (population 200,000) is one of Thailand's biggest cities. The long eastern flank of Ubon borders Laos, which gives the local culture a strong Lao flavour, while its southern tip abuts Cambodia. Although the region was once under the dominance of the ancient Khmer little evidence remains today, and Ubon city is interesting only as a major commercial centre. The one real distinguishing feature of the province is the Mun river and its junction with the Mekong. This affords some

picturesque scenery and, at the nearby cliff of Pha Taem, examples of prehistoric rock painting believed to be some 3,000 years old. Local culture receives an airing in the Candle Festival which celebrates the start of the annual Buddhist Rains Retreat.

Surin and Si Saket Sandwiched between Buriram and Ubon Ratchathani, these two provinces border Cambodia and numerous 11th- and 12th-century Khmer monuments dot the area. The finest of the ruins is Khao Phra Viharn which straddles the Cambodian border in Si Saket. Some years ago ownership of the site was the subject of international arbitration, which awarded the monument to Thailand. In recent years, however, the fighting between Khmer Rouge guerrillas and Cambodian government forces have made the area unsafe. Surin's claim to fame is its annual Elephant Round-Up, an extravaganza rather than a true round-up, which celebrates the role of the elephant in Thai life and the fact that elephant hunting was once a prime occupation of the local Suay people.

THE SOUTH

Ratchaburi Geographically part of the central region, Ratchaburi none the less lies on the way south from Bangkok. Settlement of the area dates back to ancient times, although today the province is best known for its production of earthenware jars, and for Damnoen Saduak Floating Market, an example of traditional-style commerce conducted from sampans plying small canals and now a popular tourist attraction.

Phetchaburi The popular Cha-am beach resort, on the western shore of the Gulf of Thailand, tends to overshadow the historical and cultural significance of the province. Phetchaburi town, today a small and somewhat scruffy provincial centre, has a distinguished history, first as an outpost of the ancient Khmer, then as a centre of artistic production during Ayutthaya times (the

There are no roads or vehicles on Koh Phi Phi Don, one of the South's loveliest islands. Instead, boats transport visitors around the island to the many idyllic bays and to the nearby coral reefs to dive and snorkel.

temples of Wat Yai Suwannaram and Wat Ko Keo Suttharam contain some fine mural paintings). During the Bangkok period King Mongkut (1851–68) built a hilltop palace on the outskirts of the town. The province also boasts the natural attraction of Kaeng Krachan National Park, Thailand's largest protected area covering 2,920 square kilometres (1,127 square miles) of well-watered forested hills and valleys bordering Myanmar (Burma) to the west and home to at least 40 mammal species, including Malaysian Sun Bear, Asiatic Black Bear, Clouded Leopard, Leopard, Tiger and Elephant. The park also encompasses the scenic 45-square-kilometre (17-square-mile) Kaeng Krachan Reservoir.

Prachuap Khiri Khan This narrow coastal province, directly south of Phetchaburi and bordered on the east by the Gulf of Thailand and by Myanmar (Burma) to the west, is similarly best known for a beach resort. Hua Hin is the country's oldest seaside vacation centre, first coming into vogue in the 1920s as a royal summer retreat. In spite of now catering to the international visitor, Hua Hin continues to retain much of its traditional character, as does the rest of this province of tiny fishing ports and pineapple plantations. The coastal environment is preserved at Khao Sam Roi Yot

(Mountain of 300 Peaks) National Park which, in an area of just 98 square kilometres (38 square miles) contains a wide selection of shoreline habitats — limestone hills, marshes, mangroves, coves and caves. The fauna is especially rich in birds, of which more than 300 species are to be found.

Chumphon and Ranong The geography and climate which most typically characterizes southern Thailand begins with these two provinces lying, respectively, on the east and western sides of the peninsula. Higher than average rainfall produces lusher, greener vegetation, and the limestone outcrops which are features of much of the southern landscape become noticeable. Ethnic differences, witnessed in dialect, for example, also become apparent. Situated more than 500 kilometres (300 miles) from Bangkok and north of the country's most famous beach resorts, the area is comparatively undeveloped, and Chumphon in particular has a number of unspoilt beaches and offshore islands. In Ranong, the border with Myanmar (Burma), which until now has occupied the western side of the peninsula, ends and Thailand's Andaman Sea coast begins. With much of its area taken up with hills and forest, Ranong has the distinction of being the nation's least populated province.

Phang-Nga The province is an area of tin mining, mangroves, evergreen forest and limestone karst outcrops which produce a haunting scenery of weirdly shaped hills. The geological phenomenon is most spectacular at Phang-Nga Bay where the karst formations rise above the sea as hundreds of tiny islands, all differently shaped, some humped, some sheer. Phang-Nga Bay and the Surin and the Similan island groups off the Andaman coast are today protected as marine parks.

Phuket Shaped like an irregular pearl and measuring approximately 21 kilometres wide by 48 kilometres (13 x 30 miles) long, Phuket is Thailand's largest island (albeit attached to the mainland by a causeway), and is a province in its own right. Sparsely populated outside Phuket town, the landscape is one of lush green hills, coconut groves, rubber plantations and a coastline dotted with a dozen superb beaches. Over the last decade the island has undergone enormous tourism development to rank today as the country's premier beach resort. Fame and wealth are not new, however. The island was known to early Arab and Indian seafarers and, in the 16th and 17th centuries, to various Western explorers and traders. In the 19th century Phuket prospered when tin mining boomed following a huge influx of Chinese immigrants. Today, with the tin deposits mostly depleted, rubber and tourism are the principal sources of wealth, maintaining Phuket's standing as Thailand's richest province.

Culturally the island has over the centuries been a melting pot, blending Thai, Chinese and Muslim traditions. Lifestyles vary from those of the rural Thai and the Muslim fishing communities to the commercial pursuits of the Chinese.

Krabi This is arguably the most beautiful province in the entire South. Located south of Phang-Nga and east of Phuket, it has a magnificent coastline where karst formations form a dramatic backdrop to quiet coves sheltering pristine beaches, while inland are the largest tracts of what remains of Thailand's lowland rainforests. Notable preserved areas are Koh Phi Phi-Had Nopparat National Park and Khao Panom Bencha National Park. With dramatic cliffs

Koh Phi Phi is one of the world's most beautiful island groups, although tourism development has caused some degradation of the marine environment. Khao Phanom Bencha is small — just 50 square kilometres (20 square miles) — but is a key conservation area, its rainforest supporting 156 bird species and 32 types of mammals.

Surat Thani Facing the Gulf of Thailand, Surat Thani is the largest province in the South. The area once formed part — and may have been the centre — of the Mahayana Buddhist Srivijaya empire (8th–13th centuries). Finds from the archaeological site of Chaiya, of which the best pieces are now displayed in Bangkok's National Museum, indicate cultural achievement of a high order. Historical interest is lacking in Surat Thani town, and the attraction of this commercial centre and port, supported by trade in rubber and coconut, lies in its typical southern character. The place is also the ferry point for Koh Samui, Thailand's third largest island (247 square kilometres/95 square miles) and now a beach destination rivalling Phuket in popularity. Ang Thong National Marine Park, comprising an archipelago of some 40 islands north-west of Samui, and Khao Sok National Park, on the mainland, are important conservation areas, the latter being one of the places in the country where tigers possibly still exist.

Nakhon Si Thammarat The provincial capital of Nakhon Si Thammarat, the South's second largest city (after Hat Yai), is the cultural heart of the region. Originally known as Ligor, the town dates back to the 2nd century AD and subsequently gained importance as a staging post on the early trade route between China and southern India. It was through Nakhon Si Thammarat that Theravada Buddhism spread from Sri Lanka to Sukhothai in the 13th century, and the place remains a major religious centre, the reputedly 1,000-year-old Wat Phra Mahathat being one of the South's most revered temples. Various regional arts and crafts, such as shadow puppets and niel-

loware (alloy inlaid in silver or gold objects), also continue to flourish here. Aside from the eastern coastline, the province is mountainous and forested, and the 570-square-kilometre (220-square-mile) Khao Luang National Park, encompassing the peninsula's highest peak (1,835 metres/6,020 feet), provides habitats for some 200 bird, 90 mammal and 31 reptile species.

Phattalung From mountains, forests and high plateau in the west, the eastern side of Phattalung slopes down to the upper shores of Songkhla Lake. Thale Noi Waterbird Sanctuary, a large lagoon which connects to the lake, is a protected area for 182 species of waterbird. Culturally, Phattalung

The people of Narathiwat, Thailand's most southern province, are largely Muslim. Mosques and minarets attest to their cultural links with neighbouring Malaysia.

is distinguished as the original home of two famous southern entertainments, *Manhora* dance and Thai shadow play.

Songkhla The province had the odd distinction of its administrative capital not being the major town. The brash and bustling commercial centre of Hat Yai, the South's business and communications hub, has that distinction, but Songkhla town is

the more interesting. Today a small, relaxed coastal resort located on a peninsula between the sea and the southern end of Songkhla lake, the town dates back to the 8th century and has a long history as a trading port, the legacy of which survives in traces of old architecture and a population mix of Thai, Chinese and ethnic Malay.

Trang Lying west of Phattalung and facing the Andaman Sea coastline, Trang is geographically an extension of Krabi, featuring a coast of beaches and islands, and an interior of limestone hills and lush vegetation. Historically, however, Trang was important as a communication link on the old trade route to Nakhon Si Thammarat. Modern economic activity revolves around rubber, oil palms and fishing.

Southernmost Provinces Thailand's four southernmost provinces — Satun on the west of the peninsula, Pattani, Yala and Narathiwat — are noticeably influenced by their proximity to neighbouring Malaysia. The population is more Muslim than Buddhist, and mosques rather than temples are the cultural sights — Pattani Central Mosque being the largest in Thailand. Geographically, the Gulf of Thailand shores of Pattani and Narathiwat feature some splendid beaches that are completely undeveloped, while landlocked Yala is characterized by a landscape of mainly mountains and forests, although rubber production makes it the most prosperous and fastest developing province in the far south. Satun, small and remote, facing the Andaman Sea, boasts two major wildlife reserves, Tarutao Marine National Park and Thale Ban National Park. The former, located 31 kilometres (19 miles) off the coast and clustered around 51 islands, combines magnificent scenery with a wealth of marine life, including a wide variety of corals. The 102 square kilometres (39 square miles) of Thale Ban National Park encompass the extraordinary richness of southern rainforests that once covered the peninsula.

HIGHLANDS AND HILLTRIBES

NORTHERN THAILAND

Northern Thailand stands apart from other regions of the country as an area of forested highlands traversed by parallel river valleys. The region boasts the country's highest peak, Doi Inthanon, while other upland ranges, although all well below the tree-line, present a picturesquely rugged landscape, parts of which are still comparatively remote. This

is also teak country where work elephants once played an important role in the extraction of logs, but over-exploitation has led to extensive deforestation resulting in the introduction of a logging ban in 1989, legislation that unfortunately came too late to save the finest teak reserves.

It is not only geography that distinguishes the North; history, cultural traditions and ethnic make-up all contribute to a distinct identity. From the late 13th century until the early 1900s the region was largely independent, in its early heyday a thriving kingdom known as Lanna, 'the land of a million rice fields'. Autonomous development, coupled with strong influences from neighbouring Laos and, most especially, Burma (now Myanmar), resulted in distinctive northern arts and architecture. Notably, the temples of Chiang Mai, formerly the capital of Lanna and today Thailand's unofficial second city, are not only far older than those of Bangkok, they are also different in style and decorative detail. Northern handicrafts, too, have remained a thriving tradition, and skills in woodcarving, silverware, celadon pottery and

lacquerware continue to flourish.

Proud of their own heritage, Northerners tend to remain more faithful to long-held values than their Bangkok counterparts and are generally home-loving, thrifty and wary of spending money ostentatiously. The custom of entering the monkhood is still widespread among boys and young men, and ordination ceremonies are particularly elaborate. Festivals in the North are celebrated with greater panache and exuberance than elsewhere in the country, and the local cuisine, with a strong Burmese influence, is a notable treat even in a land renowned for its culinary arts.

The region is strongly coloured by ethnic minorities, hilltribes who continue to pursue independent lifestyles outside mainstream society. Inevitably, the modern world is now beginning to encroach upon tribal ways, yet hilltribe villages with their typically costumed inhabitants continue to characterize much of the northern landscape.

Along with the rest of the country, the North is today changing under the influence of Thailand's recent economic boom years. Chiang Mai, the region's largest city and focal point, is no longer the quaint backwater it once was. Less altered, however, are historic towns such as Chiang Rai, Chiang Saen and Nan, while sleepy highland settlements like Mae Hong Son retain a character all their own, hidden in valleys surrounded by timeless hills.

The focal point of the North is Chiang Mai. It is popularly regarded as the capital of the region, a status arising out of the city's original role as the power centre of the ancient Lanna kingdom which for centuries held sway over most of what is now northern Thailand. Not until early in the present century did Chiang Mai become fully under the control of the central government. Although modern development today extends well beyond the old city walls and the banks of the Ping river (below left), Chiang Mai remains steeped in history. King Mengrai, who founded the city in the late 13th century, remains much revered and is honoured in statues and festival parades, often depicted with his two famous allies, the kings of Sukhothai and Phayao (left). With a largely separate historical development the North has evolved its own art and architectural styles, and venerable temples such as Wat Phra Singh (below) are distinct from those found further south. Not only temple forms, but also decorative motifs, especially woodcarving, along with mural paintings and sculpture, all display characteristics which are unique to the region.

PREVIOUS PAGES

Page 50: Travel in northern Thailand presents stunning vistas of high, forested hills and lush, fertile valleys. Tucked away in this idyllic landscape are rural villages such as Pong Yeang, where the way of life has altered little over the centuries.

Page 51: Traditionally costumed Hmong (Meo) hilltribe people, and other tribal minorities who inhabit the highlands, add a dash of exotic colour to the landscape.

Encounters with the past are inescapable in Chiang Mai. Among the city's many historic buildings, Wat Chiang Man (right) is widely regarded as the oldest. But the distinction of Chiang Mai is not limited to its history; the people and the traditions they preserve equally set the place apart. Festivals are loved by all Thais but no one celebrates them with more style and panache than the northerners. In addition to national celebrations, the North boasts numerous annual festive occasions of its own. Among the most spectacular is the Flower Festival in which gorgeously decorated floral floats (above) are paraded through the city.

Not only the commercial and administrative centre of the North, Chiang Mai is also very much the region's cultural heart, something that is equally visible by night as by day. A big attraction for all travellers is the city's famed Night Market *(opposite, below right), a veritable shopper's paradise. As fascinating for the browser as for the dedicated bargain-hunter, the market presents a dazzling array of Chiang Mai's renowned handicrafts, along with inexpensive clothing, souvenirs and the distinctive silver jewellery and intricate embroidery of the hilltribe minorities. Cultural performances, such as the dance dramas relating the history of King Mengrai and his allies (opposite, above) and firework displays (opposite, below left) at* Loy Krathong *and other annual festivals are also part of a night-time scene that captures both a sense of tradition and a typically northern propensity for having fun.*

The northern adherence to tradition also has a serious side. For example, candlelit processions are held to commemorate the major Buddhist holidays, the holiest of which is *Visaka Puja, honouring the birth, enlightenment and death of the Lord Buddha, seen here at Wat Chedi Luang (right). While such events are customary throughout the country, celebrations tend to be more elaborate in Chiang Mai.*

Chiang Mai is possibly the world's largest centre for cottage industries. Scattered in and around the city are countless workshops producing a wide variety of handicrafts, ranging from silk fans (above left) to woodcarving, silverware, celadon pottery and hand-woven cloth. Designs are both traditional and modern, although the means of production remain largely unchanged, having been handed down from generation to generation. Old-fashioned hand looms (left) may look primitive but in the hands of a skilled weaver they can produce superb quality cloth. Both silk and cotton are woven in Chiang Mai, and while the material is traditionally used for clothing, it has in modern times also become popular with interior designers.

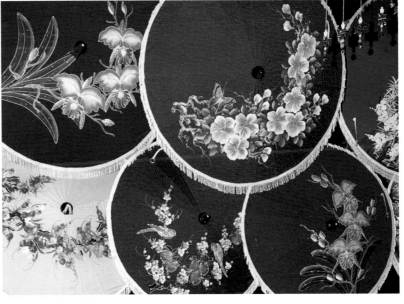

Most striking of all Chiang Mai's handicrafts are hand-painted umbrellas (above and right) *which are the speciality of Bor Sang village. So typical and so colourful are the umbrellas that they are often prominently featured in local festivals* (top).

Northern Thailand's religious and domestic architecture is special to the region in terms of both design and decoration. Northern or Lanna-style temples are most readily characterized by their typically sturdy chedis, as exemplified at the hilltop Wat Phra That Doi Suthep (above) located on the north-western outskirts of Chiang Mai. When compared with the more obviously ornate and somewhat stereotyped religious architecture further south, Lanna temples have a refreshing intimacy and naivety, their sturdy, squat proportions graced by low sweeping roofs and a sense of openness enhanced by the liberal use of wood. Domestic architecture likewise takes advantage of the North's once abundant supply of teak. It lacks the rich decorative detail of the temple, instead deriving its imposing form from complex multi-gabled roofs (left) which bear the unmistakable Lanna device of the galae, crossed gable ends in carved wood. Open verandahs add a sense of spaciousness, outdoor areas being an integral part of the living space.

As fascinating as Lanna temples and other monuments are, it is the natural scenery and cameo sights of rural life that make the northern experience so rewarding. Chiang Mai may be a city but the countryside is right on its doorstep and there is every opportunity to get out and about and sample the pleasure of a still largely undisturbed natural landscape. The Ping, one of the North's principal rivers, flows through Chiang Mai and yet only a few kilometres away the riverine scene reverts to its pristine state, best appreciated by taking a leisurely trip on a bamboo raft (right). An enduring figure in the northern landscape is the elephant. Long domesticated as work animals, elephants' strength as well as sure-footed movement in the confined space of hillside forests make them essential partners of man in the extraction of teak. Today, with a drastic decline in teak stands, logging is banned, although elephants continue to display their skills at Chiang Dao and other training camps in the Chiang Mai area. Oddly, elephants suffer from the heat and bathing in the river (below left) is part of the essential care of the animals.

With rural communities by and large continuing to cling to unchanging lifestyles, travel in the North provides unexpected glimpses of time-honoured practices. Manifestations of traditional rites, as seen in this decorated funeral carriage (below right), attest to cultural patterns undimmed by time and modern development.

Chiang Mai does not have a monopoly on historic temples, and nearby Lamphun and Lampang, south of the city, are both ancient towns with monuments bearing witness to a long and illustrious past. Standing on the site of Lamphun's former royal palace, Wat Phra That Haripunchai (right) has been rebuilt several times over the centuries, although it is none the less impressive. The large temple complex shelters a school for young Buddhist monks (left).

Further south, on Highway I, Lampang boasts a number of venerable temples displaying Burmese as well as Thai architectural styles. However, its most important monument, Wat Phra That Lampang Luang, lies several kilometres outside town. Long ago a fortified site, the temple compound is striking both for its layout and the detail of its shrines (above, left and right).

Travelling north-west of Chiang Mai, towards the Myanmar border, the hill scenery becomes wilder and lusher. Clearings on the forested hillsides mark the villages and rice fields of the Hmong (Meo) and other hilltribes (left), *while cultivated flowers (opposite, below) blossom in the near temperate climate of the North.* The focal point of the region is the little town of Mae Hong Son which occupies an idyllic valley surrounded by high hills.

Virtually cut off from the rest of the country until the 1960s, Mae Hong Son retains a character of its own, defined by the Burmese-influenced architecture of temples such as Wat Chong Kam (above). The customs of the local Thai Yai, or Shan, people are also distinct, most readily witnessed in the colourful Poy Sang Long ordination ceremony for young boys (above left and opposite, above right) *held in April.*

Adding colour and cultural diversity to the North are the hilltribe minorities who inhabit the jungle-covered mountain slopes and maintain largely independent lifestyles in their own quasi-autonomous villages. It is estimated that there are around 550,000 tribespeople in the region, most belonging to one of seven principal groups – Karen, Hmong (Meo), Akha, Lahu, Lawa, Lisu and Yao. Each group is culturally and linguistically distinct, although differences are most visible in the traditional costumes, as seen in (opposite, left, top to bottom), Yao, Hmong, Akha and (above) Lisu girls.

Unmistakable among the smaller tribal groups are the Padaung, a subgrouping of the Karen commonly called 'Long-necks' on account of the fashion among the women to wear brass rings around their necks (opposite, below right) – a practice which depresses the collar bone rather than stretches the neck. The Padaung more typically inhabit Myanmar, but in recent years a few have migrated across the border into Mae Hong Son province. Tourism has now caught up with the hilltribes and most villages these days will have a souvenir stall, pictured here (opposite, above right) run by a Yao couple. Yet the old ways have not died out totally and winnowing (above right), weaving (below right) and other chores are all part of the daily scene in Karen and other hilltribe villages.

65

Perhaps the most famous location in the North is the 'Golden Triangle', lying due north of Chiang Mai in Chiang Rai province. The name refers generally to where much of the world's opium comes from – an area stretching well beyond Thailand west into Myanmar and east across the Mekong into Laos (left). More specifically, the 'Golden Triangle' denotes the point where the borders of the three countries meet at the junction of the Mekong river and its tiny Ruak tributary.

Appearing little developed yet easily accessible, Chiang Rai lends itself to soft adventure travel, whether trekking through the hills in hilltribe country (opposite, below left), or having a raft custom built (above) for a cruise down the Kok river. Alternatively, the market at the border town of Mae Sai (opposite, above), Thailand's northernmost point, or Wat Pa Sak and other ancient ruins at Chiang Saen (opposite, below right) hold their own attractions.

Thai rural life continues to revolve around the observance of religious rites, and in the far North the temple is where time-honoured customs are most readily witnessed. The splendid façade of Wat Pasaknoi, near Chiang Saen, for example, provides the perfect backdrop for a traditional dance performance enacted during a purification ceremony (top).

Temples have always been supported by local fund-raising activities, although now modern pick-up trucks (above) are more likely to bear the typical offerings than the buffalo carts of old. Whole communities dressed according to custom will form processions (right) and parade through village streets on the way to the temple to celebrate important Buddhist festivals and rituals.

Compared to other parts of the North, Nan is the least visited. Tucked away in the valley of the river of the same name, it lies off the beaten track and the only time it draws attention to itself is during its annual boat racing festival (above). Held in October to mark the end of the annual rains, the regatta is a thrilling affair with teams of oarsmen from all over the province gathering to vie for the honours. But Nan is also a historic town and Wat Chang Kham Vora Viharn (left) and a number of other venerable temples rank among the North's most intriguing monuments.

Founded in the mid 14th century and once the capital of an independent principality, Nan preserves to a remarkable degree testaments to its long and colourful past. The town was conquered in 1449 by King Tilokaraja of Chiang Mai who ordered the casting of a 4.1-m (13½-ft) high bronze Buddha to commemorate the event. Known as Phra Chao Thong Tip, this excellent example of Sukhothai-style sculpture (right) *is today enshrined in Wat Suan Tan.*

Fine mural paintings in Wat Phumin (below) *also attest to Nan's cultural attainment, while housed in a small but well-kept museum is the town's most famous relic, a black elephant tusk* (below right), *reputedly presented to the local ruler some 300 years ago. Surprisingly, Nan's wealth of sights is masked by its unpretentious streets* (bottom), *which lend an inescapable charm to what is undoubtedly one of the North's forgotten treasures.*

Hmong tribespeople don their finery to celebrate the New Year (this page and opposite), one of the most important events in their calendar. It is scenes such as these which typify northern Thailand and, while change is inevitably catching up with the region, the villages of both rural Thai communities and the tribal minorities still present a picture of timeless ways. Northerners relish their unique history and heritage, and appear largely reluctant to abandon time-honoured customs and beliefs in favour of any headlong dash into the 21st century. Such confidence in a separate identity is what ultimately characterizes the North, a region different not only in its topography but also in its customs and culture.

Referred to in Thai as the Meo, the Hmong (the name they call themselves, which translates as 'Free People') are a large group scattered widely over the northern regions. Their dress is striking, consisting traditionally of dark cloth lavished with much colourful embroidery and appliqué, especially on lapels, armbands, cuffs and sashes. Also traditional is the heavy silver jewellery, often constituting a family's wealth, worn mainly by the women but, for special occasions, by the men as well (right). Hilltribe costume and handicrafts have become immensely popular tourist purchases. They can be bought not just from village stalls all over the North but now, in a thriving commercial market, also in big city shops.

THE HEART OF THE KINGDOM

THE CENTRAL PLAINS AND THE WEST

Thailand's Central Plains form the heart of the Kingdom both physically and historically. It was in these fertile, well watered lands that the Thai people became united as a nation, and where life was amply sustained by agricultural abundance. Stretching from the northern hills to the Gulf of Thailand in the south, the plains are dominated by the Chao Phraya, the country's major river formed by the confluence of several streams flowing out of the North. In the course of their historical development the Thais expanded the natural waterways with a network of canals which served as both irrigation channels and communication links for what has traditionally been a waterborne society.

The flat, largely featureless landscape has thus been transformed into the archetypal image of Thailand, a patchwork of paddy fields producing the bulk of the country's all-important rice crop. Scattered throughout the rural scene are villages as well as several sizeable towns, making the region the most densely populated in spite of its agricultural base.

The fertility of the land and the ease of communication afforded by the Chao Phraya river system made the Central Plains a natural site of settlement, and the region encompasses virtually all the important monuments that signpost the evolution of Thai civilization. On the northern edge stand the ruins of Sukhothai, the nation's first capital founded in the 13th century, and its contemporary satellite cities of Si Satchanalai, Phitsanulok and Kamphaeng Phet. These ancient centres form the cradle of Thai civilization, and the art and architecture evolved here constitute the first flowering of indigenous cultural forms, along with religious, social and political systems which set the pattern of nationhood.

To the west of Sukhothai lies Tak, the gateway city to the North and, beyond, Mae Sot on the Burmese border. South is Nakhon Sawan, a populous centre on the north-south trade route, while below is the focal point of Thailand's most formative historical development. Here is the site of Ayutthaya, the capital from 1350 until its destruction at the hands of the Burmese in 1767, and Lopburi, the second capital during Ayutthaya's 17th-century golden era. Both towns are today somewhat shabby provincial centres, although the ruins within their boundaries have been preserved as well as possible to offer an intriguing window on to the past.

The western edge of the Central Plains remains comparatively untouched. The flat lands give way to hills, the tail end of the northern highlands, and the countryside presents a picture of untamed jungle and prime forest cover. This is the location of Huai Kha Khaeng Wildlife Sanctuary, one of the largest and most important nature reserves in the country, where fast dwindling wildlife can still find refuge in Thailand's otherwise increasingly urbanized environment.

The Central Plains form the heart of Thailand, not only in geographical terms but also historically. It was here, on the northern edge of these fertile lowlands, that the nation first came into existence as a sovereign state in the 13th century at Sukhothai, the original capital of the newly united Thais. The chedis *and other temple ruins of this once glorious city are today preserved at Sukhothai Historical Park* (opposite), *Thailand's premier historical site. Dominating the site is Wat Mahathat* (above left), *noted for its lotus-bud* chedi, *an architectural style unique to the period, and its decorative detail* (above right). *To the north is Si Satchanalai, a satellite city, whose ruins are smaller although arguably more evocative than those of Sukhothai, notably the superb Wat Chang Lom* (right).

PREVIOUS PAGES
Page 74: *Saffron-robed monks ascend the steps to Phra Buddhabat at Saraburi, an important pilgrimage site enshrining a revered Buddha footprint.* Page 75: *At Lopburi young boys learn the martial art of kick boxing, now a popular sport but originally a form of unarmed combat taught to Thai soldiers during Lopburi's heyday in the Ayutthaya period.*

Straddling the Nan river, south-east of Sukhothai, Phitsanulok is typical of the larger towns in the upper part of the Central Plains. Drawing definition from the river, once an important communication highway, and welcoming the traveller with floating riverside restaurants (above left) and a handful of provincial hotels, the town is today a regional service centre which none the less recalls a more illustrious past. Phitsanulok rose to prominence in the late 14th and early 15th centuries, when it was a strategic point between waning Sukhothai and the rising power of Ayutthaya to the south. Dominating the town is the prang of Wat Phra Si Ratana Mahathat (above right), which dates back to the 14th century and enshrines the important late Sukhothai-style image of Phra Buddha Chinnarat (opposite).

The landscape of Thung Salaeng Luang National Park (left) also typifies the area, with the hills of the North meeting the grassy valleys at the beginning of the plains, a habitat for elephants, tigers, boar and deer, as well as nearly 200 bird species.

Lying to the west, the town of Kamphaeng Phet stands on the banks of the Ping river and is a riverine settlement similar to Phitsanulok, also tracing its history back to the Sukhothai era when it was a front-line defence against the forces of Ayutthaya. Echoes of the past survive in the weathered statuary of Wat Phra Keo (opposite) and the evocative ruins of other early temples. A more modern claim to fame is Kamphaeng Phet's Banana Festival (below right), held annually in September and featuring floats fabulously fashioned out of the fruit.

Heading further west, beyond Tak, a ridge of mountains separates the upper plains from the valley of the Moei river which forms the boundary between Thailand and Myanmar. The Thai border town of Mae Sot is a bustling commercial centre (right) for cross-river trade (below), an activity that will shortly be greatly facilitated by the completion of a long-delayed bridge over the Moei river.

As well as being the historical heart of the nation, the Central Plains region is also the cradle of Thai culture. Although the nation's full cultural heritage owes its richness to a wealth of regional influences, the central area tends to dominate in any assessment of essential 'Thai-ness'. The dialect of the region, for example, is generally taken as the norm for the Thai language. Moreover, the art and architectural styles which blossomed at Sukhothai, as well as the religious, social and political systems first devised there, set a pattern which has been modified over the centuries but not altered in its essentials. The most visible manifestations today of the local culture specific to the Central Plains are music and dance. Lopburi, an important power centre both in the pre-Thai Khmer period and the Ayutthaya era, is reflected in the name of the Ram Lopburi dance (left), while traditional orchestras (below right) and such instruments as the chakay (below left) still accompany dance performances.

A vast repertoire of popular folk dances originated in the Central Plains and continue to be performed today. Mangklala Long Drum Dance (above) and the Ram Koam Lantern Dance (right) are widely performed both in the provinces and at cultural shows in Bangkok. Brightly coloured costumes are integral to any dance performance, adding visual vibrancy to the display of studied and highly stylized movement.

Not only the dances themselves, but the occasions or actions they celebrate also tend to either have their origins in or in some way relate to the broader culture of the Central Plains. The Ram Koam Lantern Dance (right), for example, is popular at Loy Krathong, an enchanting festival to honour the mother of waters, which is widely believed to have been first celebrated in its inimitable Thai form at Sukhothai in the late 13th century.

The importance of the Central Plains is due ultimately to geography. As with the rise of all early civilizations, that of the Thai was first dependent on agricultural production. Without the means to sustain an army that could defend its borders and a large workforce able to construct its monuments, the nation could not have blossomed. The fertile, well-watered plains fulfilled the necessary preconditions, the land supporting wet-rice cultivation and the lakes and rivers providing fish, the principal source of protein in the Thai diet. Much the same prevails today and the Central Plains are still the nation's rice bowl. Tending the rice fields is laborious work (above) that has scarcely altered over the years, and virtually every task is done by hand, from planting out the seedlings at the start of the rainy season in June to harvesting in December or January. Only recently have small hand-held mechanical ploughs started to replace water buffalo drawing a simple share.

Workers returning home at the end of the day (left), a fisherman on Bung Boraphet lake, near Nakhon Sawan, at sunset (opposite), and other repeated scenes reinforce the sense of an unchanging pattern of life in the Central Plains.

West of the Central Plains, the land rises in the area towards the Myanmar border and the scene shifts from the cultivated neatness of the paddy fields to a wilder, more rugged natural beauty. Here, at Thung Yai and Huai Kha Khaeng Wildlife Sanctuaries (above left) and in the area around Umphang are to be found the best tracts of tropical broadleaf forest still surviving in the country. These sanctuaries shelter a large number of plant and animal species that have vanished elsewhere.

As in other parts of the world, Thailand's wildlife has suffered from massive deforestation, and yet there remains an exotic variety of flora and fauna. Dendrobium cariniferum (top) is but one of more than 1,000 species of orchids, while an extraordinary natural diversity is nowhere more apparent than in the insect life, among which there are an estimated 10,000 species of beetles and some 1,200 butterflies (above right). Thailand is also particularly rich in bird life, with well over 900 species, including the Wreathed Hornbill (left), which is just one of 12 species of hornbill found in the country.

With densely forested hills, rivers and waterfalls, the natural scenery around Umphang (above) ranks as arguably the most stunningly beautiful in the whole of the country. In spite of the loss of primary forest cover, Thailand still offers enormous scope for appreciating the bounty of nature. Over 10 per cent of the world's known animals are found here, including at least 280 mammal species, among which is the Tiger (right), Asia's largest species of wild cat. Now endangered animals, tigers are wary and shy, and not easily seen, although it is likely that the protected forests of Huai Kha Khaeng may shelter more of them than anywhere else in Thailand, due to plentiful sources of water, abundant prey and a higher level of conservation.

Towards the lower end of the Central Plains, in the regions alongside the Chao Phraya river, the sights and scenes become more varied as reminders both of the country's long history and its defining cultural patterns blend in a kaleidoscope of images. The most fascinating town before one reaches the all-important former capital of Ayutthaya is Lopburi. Today a rather uninspiring provincial centre, Lopburi experienced its golden era in the 17th century when King Narai made the town his second capital. The ruins of his palace, approached through massive gateways (left), conjure a good impression of former magnificence.

South of Lopburi, the important Holy Footprint shrine of Phra Buddhabat at Saraburi presents emotive cameos of Buddhist devotion, especially during major festive days such as Khao Pansa (opposite, top left) and in details such as touching the temple bells to make merit (opposite, top right). Elsewhere, the scenes range from the ubiquitous kerbside food stalls (above), so typical of the Thai urban landscape, to the startling fairy-tale-like architecture of Bang Pa-in. A royal summer palace, Bang Pa-in is extraordinary in its eclectic mix of buildings. A Chinese pagoda (opposite, below left) and a superb Thai-style pavilion (opposite, below right) are contrasted by other structures with a European look, which reflect a widespread Thai fascination with Western styles at the turn of the 20th century.

Ayutthaya, some 70 kilometres (40 miles) north of Bangkok, is the real showcase of Thai history, its Buddha statuary (above left) and superb chedis (left) *recalling the classic period when Thailand was known as Siam. The city was founded in the 14th century and remained the capital for over 400 years until its destruction by the Burmese in 1767. Located on the banks of the Chao Phraya river at its junction with two tributaries, it was designed in the traditional Thai fashion as an island city, surrounded by water and criss-crossed by canals which served as the main streets. With magnificent palaces and gilded temples, Ayutthaya was during its 17th-century heyday the most magnificent and most powerful metropolis in the Orient.*

Although the Burmese defeat of Ayutthaya left the city in ruins, the remains, mostly of temples, that have survived give an inkling of past greatness. Devotion to Ayutthaya is seen in robes draped over a row of Buddha images at Wat Phra Mongkol Bopit (above) as a mark of respect, and the site continues to be held sacred by the Thais for both its religious and historical importance. The ruins display various architectural styles evolved during different periods. The distinctive rounded prangs (right) featured in some major temple compounds, including that of Wat Mahathat, one of Ayutthaya's most impressive monuments, stand in contrast to the more common bell-shaped chedis. The prang is actually a Khmer architectural form and it is illustrative of the fact that the former Thai capital was in many ways the cultural heir of Angkor, the ancient Khmer power centre which the Thais conquered in the 15th century.

GATEWAY TO THE NATION

BANGKOK AND THE SURROUNDING AREA

Thailand's capital, the first sight of the country for most visitors, scarcely matches any preconceived ideas of a fabled city of the Orient, the 'Venice of the East' as it was once known. A few canals do survive, but today's Bangkok appears as a huge concrete sprawl of paved streets bristling with high-rises and clogged with some of the worst traffic congestion in the world. However, beneath the modern and ostensibly western veneer lie captivating sights of temples, palaces, markets and other typically Thai scenes in which the old manages to coexist with the new.

Founded as the capital in 1782, Bangkok is a relatively young city. It has also borne the brunt of Thailand's economic growth and so displays more of the stresses and strains of rapid development than other parts of the country. Beyond the sprawl of the metropolitan area the landscape quickly reverts to a more traditional picture in which a sense of history and natural splendour combine to present images of classic Thailand.

A short distance to the west is Nakhon Pathom, one of the country's oldest settlements and site of what was a Mon capital during the Dvaravati period (6th–11th centuries) and the earliest known centre of Buddhist learning in Thailand. The present town is dominated by the Phra Pathom Chedi, the world's tallest Buddhist monument, which marks the location of an ancient *chedi* that was destroyed in the 11th century.

Further west, modern history is vividly recalled at Kanchanaburi where the infamous Bridge over the River Kwai was constructed by allied POWs of the Japanese during World War II. It is an evocative spot, the memory of those who died working on the bridge surviving in two immaculately kept war cemeteries and a museum. Contrasting with tragic history is the natural beauty of Kanchanaburi province, an area in which jungle-clad hills, wooded river valleys, caves and waterfalls offer some of the most picturesque scenery to be found anywhere in the country.

Different yet equally traditional scenes lie immediately south of Bangkok, with small fishing towns interspersed with shrimp farms strung out along the coast of the Gulf of Thailand. Places of note include Ratchaburi, famed for water jars and other ceramic products, while among tourist sights are a huge crocodile farm and the Ancient City where many of the country's most famous historic buildings have been reconstructed in authentic scale models.

East of the capital leads towards the Khorat Plateau and the vast semi-arid region of I-san. Before this poor rural district is reached is Khao Yai, Thailand's oldest established national park and one of the richest in flora and fauna. The park is remarkable equally for its stunning natural beauty and its wildlife population which includes elephants, tigers, leopards, bears and various species of deer.

Bangkok is today a huge, sprawling modern metropolis lacking any easily discerned downtown area, but the original core of the old royal city still marks a symbolic centre. Located on the east bank of the Chao Phraya, at a spot where the river makes a broad curve, the area is known as Ratanakosin Island and was indeed originally an island when concentric canals linking with the river formed a ring of outer defences. Here are located all the major historical buildings dating from the founding of the city in 1782 and incorporating the regal prestige and capital status recreated after the loss of Ayutthaya. Most famous of all are the Grand Palace (above left) and Wat Phra Keo, Temple of the Emerald Buddha (left and opposite). Both date from the founding of Bangkok as the capital, although the collection of regal apartments that form the Grand Palace was added to by successive monarchs. No longer the official residence of the King, the Palace continues to be used for state functions, and Wat Phra Keo remains the royal chapel. Enshrined in the temple is the statue of the Emerald Buddha (above right), the nation's most sacred image. The statue has three bejewelled costumes, one for each season, which are changed at the appropriate time by the King.

PREVIOUS PAGES
Page 92: The Chao Phraya river was originally Bangkok's main artery. Long since expanding away from the river, the modern city has in recent years returned attention to this historic heart which now bristles with concrete and glass high-rises. Page 93: In classical dance performances and in countless other cultural manifestations Bangkok manages to preserve the old along with the new.

Amid Bangkok's welter of modern development, from glitzy department stores to gleaming office towers, the on-going observance of age-old ceremonies, rites and customs provides an all-important link with the past. One of the most cohesive forces in Thai society is the monarchy and while the government now follows a constitutional system, royal rites and pageantry are still widely featured in the national calendar. Trooping of the Colours (left) and the Ploughing Ceremony (below) are both presided over by His Majesty the King, the latter event being an ancient ritual held in May to herald the start of the rice planting season and augur well for a good harvest.

Royal Barge Processions (opposite, below left) with oarsmen in traditional costume (opposite, below right) are no longer annually staged on the Chao Phraya river as they once were, but the custom is regularly revived to mark major royal landmarks, most recently His Majesty the King's Golden Jubilee in 1996. With popular traditions, a similar adherence to the past persists, as vividly witnessed in the February to April kite-flying season when young and old alike flock to the Pramane Ground in front of the Grand Palace (opposite, above) to indulge in a long-favoured pastime.

More Buddha images are to be seen in Thailand than probably any other country in the world, and enshrined in Bangkok's numerous temples are sacred statues attesting to the faith that has underpinned the nation since its founding in the 13th century. The Reclining Buddha (above left) *at Wat Po, the city's oldest and largest temple-monastery complex, and the Golden Buddha* (above right), *a 3-m (10-ft) high solid gold image at Wat Traimit, are but two of the city's most famous Buddha statues. These are not idols, nor are they worshipped, rather they serve as reminders of the Lord Buddha's life and teaching. No sacred image is conceived or perceived as a work of art, although the craftsmanship perfected in sculpting and casting Buddha statues imbued the finest examples with a high aesthetic quality.*

Artistic skills equal to those demonstrated in statuary are evident in the architecture of Buddhist temples which, typified by Wat Arun, the Temple of Dawn (left), display a wealth of decorative detail.

Temples such as Wat Benchamabophit, the Marble Temple, (below left) are naturally the main focus of religious observance, but not exclusively so. Numerous shrines scattered around the city, such as the memorial to the younger brother of King Rama I at Wat Chana Songkhram (below right), attract devotees who present offerings of flowers, candles and incense. Buddhism is primarily concerned with man's ultimate release from suffering and does not specifically address mundane concerns. At the same time, the popular practice of Buddhism in Thailand incorporates older beliefs based in Brahmanism and animism. Accordingly, various shrines have become widely accepted as having the power to bestow good fortune or grant wishes. The most famous of these in Bangkok is the Erawan Shrine (right), which honours the Hindu god Brahma. Dating from the 1950s, the shrine was originally erected on the advice of Brahman priests to end a spate of misfortune that had plagued the construction of the now demolished Erawan Hotel. It had the desired effect and ever since the shrine has been viewed as an exceptionally potent source of good luck.

Modern prosperity has not diminished Bangkok's enthusiasm for celebrating traditional festive occasions. As in the past, it is the river which provides a city focal point, and today's deluxe hotels along the banks of the Chao Phraya recreate classic riverine settings for banquets and gala events. Open-air terraces are perfect for celebrating Loy Krathong (above left), with pools reflecting the delicate beauty of krathongs (left) and spectacular firework displays lighting up the sky (above).

Classical performing arts have lost ground to modern city entertainments, but they have not totally vanished from the urban scene, being preserved at Bangkok's National Theatre and several Thai restaurants featuring cultural shows. Most famous of the traditional dance forms is the khon *masked drama (above right), which recounts the saga of Prince Rama as described in the* Ramakien, *the Thai version of the Indian* Ramayana *epic. With a huge cast of exotic characters, the plot is involved and in the past performances could last an entire day. In modern shows only excerpts are presented in what is usually a mixed programme of* khon *(originally exclusively a royal entertainment), other styles of classical dance, such as Sukhothai (right), and regional folk dances.*

Thai style is expressed not only in temples and the classical arts, it is also widely and imaginatively applied to domestic architecture and interior design, as exemplified in the several Bangkok private homes which have been turned into museums. Suan Pakkard Palace combines traditional Thai houses, tropical gardens and a fine collection of antiques (above), while Vimanmek Mansion (left), a formal royal residence, is reputedly the world's largest golden teak building. Another excellent collection of antiques that has been built up privately is at the Prasart Museum (opposite, below left).

Foreigners have shown great appreciation of Thai style and Jim Thompson, the American businessman who revitalized the Thai silk industry in the 1950s and '60s, created a superb home in Bangkok (opposite, above and below right). He disappeared under unexplained circumstances in 1967 while vacationing in Malaysia, yet his house has been preserved as if awaiting his return.

In spite of department stores and shopping malls springing up throughout the city over the last decade, traditional markets and street stalls have not vanished from Bangkok. Fresh produce markets displaying Thailand's rich bounty of vegetables, fruit and spices (above) are intriguing for their sheer variety and volume of items. It is the ready availability of fresh ingredients that helps make Thai food such a delight. For the inveterate shopper there is nothing to beat the Weekend Market at Chatuchak Park. Held over Saturday and Sunday only, this vast market offers just about everything from antiques and bric-a-brac (left) to potted plants and pets. Originally located at the Pramane Ground, in front of the Grand Palace, the Weekend Market was moved several years ago to its present location on the city's northern outskirts, but has lost nothing of its energy and vitality.

One of Bangkok's oldest commercial centres is Chinatown (right). *Long before the city achieved capital status it was a trading post, and Chinese traders formed a sizeable portion of the population, clustered along the banks of the Chao Phraya. When the old royal city was built, these merchants were resettled in the present area of Chinatown which has retained to this day its ethnic identity and traditional specialities, notably Chinese herbs and medicines, and gold. The architecture of the area is typically that of the ultra-functional shophouses, rows of three-, four- or five-storey buildings with the open-fronted ground floor serving as the shop and the upper floors accommodating the family living quarters.*

Flower stalls (below) *are an integral feature of fresh produce markets, and are remarkable especially for gorgeous orchids which are so inexpensive that they are a common feature in house, hotel and restaurant floral decoration.*

Once known as the 'Venice of the East', Bangkok was essentially a city of waterways, and it was not until the mid 19th century that the first paved roads for wheeled traffic were constructed. Today, the motor car has taken over with a vengeance and most of the original canals have been filled in. Yet sufficient remains for the old pattern to be still visible. The Chao Phraya river continues to carry considerable traffic, whether fast longtail boats (opposite) or slow barges (below right) bringing bulk cargo down from the provinces. Many Bangkokians commute to work via water taxis that ply regular routes up and down the river, while tour boats (right) provide an easy way of taking in the riverside sights.

The canals – klongs as they are known in Thai – which were once the main streets, have mostly disappeared from Bangkok proper, but typical scenes of klong life (above) can be seen in Thonburi on the west bank of the river. Here, wooden houses face the water and the usual way of getting about is by boat. Even the shops are aquatic, with fruit, vegetable and grocery sellers peddling their goods from sampans.

Bangkok is a city of luxuries as much as it is a place of exotic sights, and it offers every opportunity for enjoying the finer things in life. Many of the capital's top hotels rank among the best in the world, with a degree of luxury and, more importantly, a level of service that are unmatched. Every city has its landmark hotel and in Bangkok it is the riverside Oriental. Fully modernized and expanded in recent decades, it dates back to the 19th century and the 'Author's Lounge' of its original wing (above) recalls the charm of a more leisured era of travel. Novelist Joseph Conrad is reputed to have dined here, thereby setting a tradition which the hotel has pursued, naming its suites after other famous literary guests from Somerset Maugham to Graham Greene and Gore Vidal. The hotel also regularly hosts visiting royalty, business tycoons and Hollywood stars.

Catering for those able to indulge expensive tastes are Bangkok's speciality antiques shops (left). Scores of establishments are scattered around the city, while one entire floor of a top shopping plaza is devoted to collector-quality antiques with prices to match.

A sybaritic city, Bangkok tempts the senses in every way, with the spicy delights of Thai cuisine (right), the gorgeous texture of Thai silks (below left), and a lively conglomeration of night-clubs and discos (below right). Some of the biggest changes the city has undergone in recent years have been in its entertainment offerings. Home-grown attractions, such as Thai kick boxing matches, classical Thai dance shows and, of course, the city's notorious go-go bars, are no longer the only night-time options. Concerts by top-name artistes, performances by visiting ballet companies and orchestras of world renown, and London theatre productions are also now periodic if not daily attractions. Shopping opportunities, too, have developed dramatically and, increasingly, international designer and well-known brand names fill store windows.

Excursions beyond Bangkok present a host of things to do and see. Just a short drive away on the city outskirts, the Rose Garden cultural centre and park offers the chance to take a ride on an elephant (left), or watch youngsters put on a display of Thai dances (below left). Alternatively, some 30 kilometres (18 miles) south of the city, there is the world's largest crocodile farm to visit at Samut Prakan, and also worth seeing nearby are replicas of Thailand's most famous monuments at the Ancient City.

A day trip south-west of Bangkok, taking an early-morning canal boat, brings one to the famous 'Floating Market' at Damnoen Saduak, where boat-shops selling all manner of produce throng the narrow waterways (opposite) and snacks can be bought from the sampans (below right).

Travelling west of Bangkok leads to Kanchanaburi, where two rivers, the Kwai Yai and Kwai Noi, flow through idyllic wooded valleys dotted with caves, waterfalls and scenic spots. Beyond, forested hills rise to a saw-tooth mountain range which forms the border with Myanmar and produces a seemingly isolated landscape of a wild and rugged grandeur. This is a historic area, long ago an invasion route for Burmese armies and, in more recent times, the location of the Death Railway and Bridge over the River Kwai (above), built by Allied POWs of the Japanese during World War II.

Besides the bridge at Kanchanaburi, poignant reminders of this dark period in history are found in more than 8,000 graves in two war cemeteries (left).

Before Kanchanaburi is reached, the road west of Bangkok passes Nakhon Pathom, site of the world's tallest Buddhist monument, Phra Pathom Chedi (above right), with a height of 120m (394ft). One of Thailand's most important places of worship, Nakhon Pathom is widely believed to have been the earliest centre of Buddhist learning in the country and the place where the religion first took root in what is now Thai soil. A chedi was originally erected here during the early Dvaravati period but was partially destroyed during a Burmese invasion in 1057 AD. In the 19th century, the present structure was raised over the ruins. Dominating its surroundings, the building is distinguished by a ringed cone atop a massive glazed tile base in the shape of an inverted bowl. The whole stands on a series of terraces and is surrounded by chapels and cloisters (above left) at the cardinal points.

Beyond the town of Nakhon Pathom, Buddhist temples (right) continue to be features throughout the beautiful province of Kanchanaburi, their highest levels often affording the best views of the countryside.

North-east of Bangkok, on the edge of the Khorat Plateau, is Thailand's first National Park, Khao Yai, established in 1962. Accessible in a longish day excursion from Bangkok, the huge park is the most visited of all the country's wildlife reserves. Among the resident fauna enjoying the protection of the park are the stately Great Hornbill (top left), White-handed Gibbons (top right) and some of Thailand's few remaining tigers (left). The exotic forest flora includes several species of brightly coloured gingers (above left and right), as well as orchids and flowering shrubs.

Contributing to Khao Yai's splendid natural beauty are high hills, forests, grassland, streams and waterfalls of which Haew Narok (opposite) is the most impressive.

TOWARDS THE MIGHTY MEKONG

NORTH-EASTERN THAILAND

Bordered to the north and east by the Mekong river and Laos, and to the south by Cambodia, the North-east is the largest of Thailand's main topographical regions covering about one-third of the country's land mass. The area comprises a semi-arid plateau with forested mountains in the north-west, where national parks such as Phu Luang and Phu Kradung contain the last remnants of what was once lush forest cover. Otherwise the North-east is intensely rural with a scattering of large towns – Khon Kaen, Ubon Ratchathani, Nakhon Ratchasima (Khorat) and Udon Thani – serving as commercial centres.

Known in Thai as I-san, the North-east is the least changed part of Thailand. The people speak their own melodious dialect, have their own distinctively spiced cuisine, and retain a characteristic hospitable and fun-loving nature. The economy is based almost entirely on agriculture and the majority of north-easterners follow agrarian lifestyles rooted in tradition and dictated by the annual seasonal cycle.

Local culture – music, folk dances, festivals and legends – is better preserved in the North-east than anywhere else in Thailand. Rural traditions are manifest in numerous annual festivals, colourful and often boisterous affairs which punctuate an otherwise arduous agricultural cycle. Among the most spectacular events is the *Bang Fai* (Rocket) Festival, held in the provincial capital of Yasothon, during which giant home-made rockets are fired into the air as an entreaty to the sky god for rains.

I-san is also significant as the location of several sites attesting to the early history of what is now Thailand. Archaeological discoveries at Ban Chiang in the 1970s produced evidence of a Bronze Age civilization that flourished over 5,000 years ago. This predates sites in China and Mesopotamia as the earliest known evidence of an agrarian, bronze-making culture. Elsewhere, prehistoric rock paintings can be seen on the cliffs at Pha Taem in Ubon Ratchathani province.

Moving into the era of recorded history, the North-east possesses the finest examples of ancient Khmer temples to be seen outside Cambodia. Best known of the ruins are the 12th-century temple complexes of Phimai and Prasat Phanom Rung. The architecture of the latter is considerably enhanced by a dominant hill-top location commanding panoramic views of the surrounding countryside.

Historical, topographic and cultural interest are combined in the towns that border the Mekong river, from Nong Khai in the north down to Mukdahan. The most noteworthy monument is Phra That Phanom, the North-east's most sacred shrine located in the small town of the same name, while virtually all the Mekong towns have temples of historic and architectural interest.

What is now north-eastern Thailand was once an outpost of the ancient Khmer empire centred on Angkor in present-day Cambodia. Prasat Phanom Rung (left), *with a monumental stairway leading to its impressive hill-top location, is just one of several ruined Khmer temples scattered throughout the region and attesting to the area's distinctive pre-Thai past.*

PREVIOUS PAGES
Page 116: *Buddha image near Ubon Ratchathani.*
Page 117: *Old-style bamboo wares for sale at That Phanom.*

Most of the North-east's Khmer temples date from the 12th century and exemplify the architectural genius of ancient Angkor, albeit on a much smaller scale. Many of the larger monuments, such as Prasat Hin Phimai (right), have been restored in recent years, although not all the work has been of even quality. Before it was restored, Muang Tam temple (above) presented an evocative picture of crumbling stonework and overgrown ruins. Fine examples of richly carved lintels and friezes can be seen at both Prasat Hin Phimai and Muang Tam.

The North-east, or I-san as it is known in Thai, occupies a semi-arid and largely deforested plateau where agricultural production from the poor soil scarcely rises above subsistence level. In this least developed region of the country, rural life is sustained mostly without the aid of modern advantages. Seasonal droughts are to be expected, and while the village pump (above right) provides a shower for youngsters, the large earthen jars seen in the background show a prudent provision for water storage. Along with the staple of rice, the North-east also produces a few cash crops, including tomatoes and other vegetables (above left) and tobacco, a common sight laid out in the sun to dry (right). Fish in rivers, streams and lakes provide the main source of protein in the north-eastern diet, and fishermen have devised numerous ways of catching them, not only with nets in various shapes (left), but also with ingeniously designed bamboo traps.

A creaking bullock cart (left) wending its way to and from the fields is an enduring image of I-san's traditional agrarian lifestyle.

120

The North-east is proud of its own rich tradition of regional arts and crafts, which are possibly less affected here by commercialism than anywhere else in Thailand. The River Fish dance (top) is just one of the many local folk dances that are performed on festive occasions. Similarly, music and song unique to the region, most famously the style known as mor-lam which calls for great skill in ad-libbing lyrics, continues to enjoy enormous popularity. Among local handicrafts are distinctive woven hats (left), and Ban Dan Kwian pottery (above), an especially sought-after ware produced near Khorat.

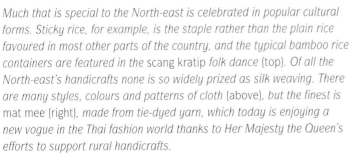

Much that is special to the North-east is celebrated in popular cultural forms. Sticky rice, for example, is the staple rather than the plain rice favoured in most other parts of the country, and the typical bamboo rice containers are featured in the scang kratip *folk dance (top). Of all the North-east's handicrafts none is so widely prized as silk weaving. There are many styles, colours and patterns of cloth (above), but the finest is* mat mee *(right), made from tie-dyed yarn, which today is enjoying a new vogue in the Thai fashion world thanks to Her Majesty the Queen's efforts to support rural handicrafts.*

The Mekong, South-east Asia's longest river, is the dominant topographical feature of the North-east. Although it does not flow through I-san, it traces almost the entire northern and eastern edges of the region, forming the border between Thailand and Laos. From the banks of its broad waters, the Mekong offers dramatic views across to Laos (right). On the Thai side, a number of largish riverine towns, such as Nakhon Phanom (top), punctuate the river's passage and serve as market towns as well as crossing points. As yet there is only one bridge across the Mekong, at Nong Khai, although there are plans for a second span to be built at Mukdahan. Otherwise, small craft (above) and flat-bottom ferries comprise what is still only light traffic on the river.

Festivals, both religious and secular, dot the calendar of the North-east to give a welcome respite from an otherwise arduous agricultural cycle. Village girls dressed in all their finery (above) and processions to village temples (left) are common sights on festive days, which the north-easterners celebrate with a joyous sense of good fun quite unparalleled in other parts of the country.

The region's biggest religious fairs are celebrated at Wat That Phanom (opposite, above) located near the banks of the Mekong on I-san's eastern edge. Dominated by a Lao-style spire, known as a that, the temple is the most sacred Buddhist shrine in the North-east, revered by both Thais and Laotians, and is honoured with traditional dances (opposite, below) and other acts of devotion during Buddhist festivals.

While all Thais love festivals, the north-easterners have their own ways of celebrating not only national events but also numerous other festive occasions that are special to the region or even to a specific town. The people of Sakon Nakhon, for example, celebrate the end of the Buddhist Rains Retreat, Ok Phansa, with boat races (above left) *and with the unique custom of fashioning miniature Buddhist temples and shrines out of beeswax* (left) *to 'make merit'. In different fashion, the beginning of the Rains Retreat, Khao Phansa, is marked in Ubon Ratchathani by the creation of huge and beautifully carved wax candles which are paraded through the town before being presented to local temples* (above).

The liveliest event in the north-eastern calendar, however, is the Rocket Festival, most elaborately celebrated at Yasothon (opposite, below). *At this time in May villagers make huge rockets by packing gunpowder into lengths of plastic tubing, some several metres long, which are launched into the air as a reminder to the sky god to send the annual rains. The two-day event is accompanied by parades, fairs and much high-spirited revelry.*

Although agriculture is the main activity of the North-east, the area none the less supports a number of large towns which serve as communication and market centres for the surrounding rural districts. Of these Khorat is the main gateway and the other big cities encountered on a roughly clockwise route are Khon Kaen, in the centre, Udon Thani and Nong Khai at the top, Nakhon Phanom to the north-east and then Ubon Ratchathani down in I-san's south-east corner. Located on the banks of the Mun river, a tributary of the Mekong, Ubon (above) boasts a few temples of interest, although its principal role is that of a commercial centre and main outlet for local produce, such as watermelons (left).

The passage of the Mun river (right) from Ubon Ratchathani to its junction with the Mekong is one of the most scenic areas in the North-east, and river resort huts (top), islands and other local beauty spots are popular excursion destinations for the townsfolk. West of Ubon, on the route back to Khorat, the town of Surin was in the past a centre for elephant training, a fact honoured today in the annual Elephant Round-up (above), an extravaganza during which the animals display their skills in forestry work and, in a reminder of former days, as mounts for warriors.

THAILAND'S RIVIERA

THE EASTERN SEABOARD

With the exception of Bangkok, the East Coast has undergone the greatest development in modern times with firstly beach resorts and latterly industrial estates transforming a once tranquil coastline.

Facing the Gulf of Thailand and forming an angled corner reaching 500 kilometres (300 miles) from the mouth of the Chao Phraya river around to the Cambodian border, the East Coast boasts several fine beaches which, along with offshore islands, make it a natural for beach resorts. The oldest of these, Bang Saen, remains popular with weekend trippers from Bangkok, but it is nearby Pattaya which was until recently Thailand's star resort. From its beginning some 30 years ago as a recreational centre for US troops on leave from Vietnam, Pattaya blossomed into an international playground, only to become a victim of its own success, eventually suffering from over-building and a poorly planned infrastructure. Quieter resorts are found further along the coast in Rayong province and on the island of Koh Samet.

If tourism first put the East Coast on the map, more recent fame and prosperity are resulting from the Eastern Seaboard Development Programme, a massive undertaking involving two large industrial estates and attendant deep-sea ports. Fuelled by natural gas from the Gulf, this zone has become a centre for Thailand's expanding petroleum products and petrochemical industries.

Away from the coast, the region's principal towns, such as Chonburi and Rayong, are unremarkable albeit bustling provincial centres. An exception is Chanthaburi, a historic and intriguing town which boasts Thailand's largest cathedral, the Church of the Immaculate Conception. Chanthaburi is also a centre for trade in the gems, especially rubies and sapphires, mined in the surrounding countryside and in neighbouring Trat province. A booming business in the 1980s, the gem market has slowed of late, although quality stones from Cambodia continue to attract dealers.

Chanthaburi and Trat are also renowned for other more obvious fruits of the earth, the countryside producing a wide variety of fresh produce including three of Thailand's most exotic fruits, durian, mangosteen and rambutan. Set against a backdrop of lush green hills, this south-eastern corner is an extremely attractive area with plantations and orchards complementing a natural landscape of considerable beauty.

Last, but by no means least, along the East Coast, is Koh Chang, Thailand's second largest island (after Phuket) and characterized by a hinterland of densely forested hills fringed by some superb beaches and coves. Koh Chang, along with other islands in the archipelago, has been designated a marine national park. Development has been slow due to difficult access, and for the moment Koh Chang remains the least spoilt of the country's tropical island hideaways.

A tiny fishing village little more than two decades ago, Pattaya Beach (left) was developed in the late 1970s and '80s as Thailand's premier seaside resort. Located on the country's eastern seaboard, it benefited from easy road access from Bangkok and boomed as an international playground in the sun. Traditional fishing vessels were turned into tour boats (above), while parasailing (opposite, above) and a host of other aquatic sports were added to offer an endless choice of activity and complement the luxury of a string of huge resort hotels (opposite, below). Today, Pattaya suffers perhaps from too much building and too little civic planning.

PREVIOUS PAGES
Page 132: Towards the border with Cambodia, Thailand's eastern coast becomes less developed and sunset over Koh Chang, the country's second largest island, presents an unspoilt scene.
Page 133: Buffalo races at Chonburi, to the north of Pattaya, are one of the few surviving traditions in an area that is becoming increasingly developed.

Originally, the beach was Pattaya's main attraction, but the development of tourism infrastructure in and around the resort has created a variety of entertainments. At Nong Nooch holiday village, just outside the town, elephant shows (above) are one of the regular attractions. For the golfer, more than half a dozen international standard courses, where both the play and the facilities are excellent, are located in the area (left).

Although Pattaya still aims to maintain its profile as a beach resort, it does, in fact, have city status and its inshore attractions vie with those of the capital. Performances of folk dances (right) and other cultural displays can be readily seen, as can the local sport of Thai kick boxing (below left), although the bouts do not attract the top fighters seen in Bangkok.

What was the original fishing village of Pattaya is today totally unrecognizable, having been transformed into what is popularly known as 'The Strip'. Here is a neon-lit fantasy world of open-air beer bars, 'go-go' bars, discos and nightclubs, all packed cheek by jowl (below right). Shopping is a further temptation, with tailors, gems and jewellery stores, and souvenir stalls all beckoning as loudly as the nightspots.

The underwater world of the Gulf of Thailand is comparatively rich in marine life, and the area is popular with snorkellers and scuba divers. Coral reefs with good populations of fish offer much to discover. Divers can expect to enjoy close encounters with such species as batfish (top) or Oriental Sweetlips (above left). A much rarer sight, and a treat for divers, is the Hawksbill Turtle (left), one of Thailand's four marine turtle species.

Not all of the eastern seaboard has succumbed to modern development and working fishing boats (above) and other traditional coastal sights are found beyond Pattaya, notably in the neighbouring province of Rayong. Most visited of the resorts on this part of the coast is Koh Samet (right), a small island noted for its sandy beaches, secluded coves and coral reefs. Long popular with budget travellers, Koh Samet is officially designated as a national park and efforts are being made to protect the environment.

Off the coast of Trat province, which abuts Cambodia, lies Koh Chang, or 'Elephant Island', the most unspoilt of all the resort areas of the eastern seaboard. With accommodation still limited to mostly thatched bungalows (left) and simple hotels with sea views (top), the island remains close to the tropical paradise of travel brochures. Visitors – few so far – can generally lay claim to nearly a whole palm-fringed beach for themselves (right), and even then there are plenty of other spots to escape to. Koh Chang itself is 30 kilometres (18 miles) long and 8 kilometres (5 miles) at its widest point, and it is only one in an archipelago of 52 islands, many of them uninhabited. Offshore, fish traps (above) attest to the unchanged lifestyle of the local people.

TROPICAL BEACHES AND OFFSHORE ISLANDS

SOUTHERN THAILAND

Forming a long narrow peninsula, southern Thailand stretches some 1,200 kilometres (750 miles) from just below Bangkok to the Malaysian border. The land is characterized by a mountainous spine and humped limestone karst formations which appear both as cliffs and offshore islets, while the coastline is indented with coves and beaches. Numerous islands, including the country's largest, Phuket, dot the coastal waters.

Topographically and, to a large extent, culturally the region divides into two, the upper and lower south. The former, which extends down to Chumphon, faces the Gulf of Thailand to the east and is bordered to the west by Myanmar (Burma). Most of the coastline is now taken over by beach resorts, notably Cha-am and Hua Hin which are within easy driving distance from Bangkok, although the traditional occupation of fishing still provides the main livelihood for the coastal villages. Away from the sea, cultivation on the narrow coastal plain is dominated by plantations, mostly pineapple.

The history of the upper south is linked closely with that of the Central Plains. The main town of the area, Phetchaburi, was an important provincial centre during the Ayutthaya and early Bangkok periods and still boasts several venerable temples, as well as a 19th-century hilltop palace built by King Rama IV. Hua Hin retains regal connections to this day, being the site of a summer palace which is still used by the Royal Family.

Beyond Chumphon, the lower south is distinguished by a more truly tropical climate and the last vestiges of Thailand's rainforests. The border with Myanmar ends near the town of Ranong and the Thai shore faces both the Andaman Sea, on the west, and the Gulf of Thailand to the east. The landscape is defined by rubber and coconut plantations which, along with tin mining in Phuket and fishing on both coasts, have been the traditional activities of the region.

The coastal ports of the lower south were once staging posts on the sea route from India to China, while the area also boasts important sites dating back to the Srivijaya period (8th–13th centuries). But although ancient settlements, such as Nakhon Si Thammarat and Songkhla, retain vestiges of the past, modern commercial development in the South is largely uninspiring, as witnessed in the region's major business hub, Hat Yai. A strong Muslim influence typifies what is a distinctive southern culture.

The lower south is best known today as the nation's top tourist attraction. Phuket island and Krabi, on the Andaman coast, and Samui island in the Gulf can all claim tropical beaches that rank among the best in the world.

Although best known for its beaches and offshore islands, the long narrow peninsula of southern Thailand displays different characteristics along its considerable length and between its western and eastern shores. The first place of note on a journey south from Bangkok is Phetchaburi. The town has a history dating back to the Khmer period and is fascinating for its several historic temples. Wat Mahathat, instantly identifiable by its striking prangs (opposite), enshrines a number of Buddha images (left), while two other temples, Wat Yai Suwannaram and Wat Ko Keo Suttharam, have some fine mural paintings. Beyond Phetchaburi, beach resorts in the upper south begin with Cha-am, a small unpretentious town with seafront shops (below left) facing a sandy beach (below).

PREVIOUS PAGES
Page 142: The white beaches and lush tropical hinterland of Koh Samui are typical of the island and the coastal scenery of the far south. Page 143: Classical Manhora dancers are part of the southern region's unique cultural tradition.

Dating back to the 1920s, Hua Hin (opposite, above) is Thailand's oldest beach resort. Located just south of Cha-am, the town is a royal summer retreat and retains a regal air even in its immaculate railway station (above).

Hua Hin's beach (right) is quiet and uncluttered, and commercial activity rises little above that of local fruit-sellers (opposite, below left). An old-style beach resort, relying on its scenery and tranquil atmosphere rather than modern watersports and nightlife, Hua Hin does none the less boast one of the country's longest-established golf courses, with girl caddies (opposite, below right), as well as deluxe accommodation ranging from a superb colonial-style hotel to the luxurious Chiva Som health spa.

147

A rich diversity of natural habitats is found in a number of national parks and wildlife reserves in southern Thailand. On the western side of the upper part of the peninsula, bordering Myanmar, Kaeng Krachan ranks as Thailand's largest national park and one of the country's most extensive and untouched tracts of evergreen rainforest (top). Backed by limestone mountains, the wetlands of Khao Sam Roi Yot National Park (right), south of Hua Hin, present a contrasting scene. Here, splay-footed Purple Swamphens (above) are among hundreds of species of birds to be seen in the area.

At Chumphon, roughly half-way down the peninsula's Gulf coast, the climate and scenery start to become more tropical. This is the beginning of Thailand's deep south, where roadside fruit stalls (left) and Pig-tailed Macaques trained to collect coconuts (above left) are ubiquitous images.

Offshore islands, such as Koh Tao, with pristine beaches (opposite, below), are more numerous along the far southern coast, and many of them are now provided with basic beach bungalows (above) that are popular with independent travellers. Surat Thani, a key town on the Gulf coast, serves as the ferry port for many of the outlying islands. During its Chak Phra festival at the end of the Buddhist Rains Retreat, revered Buddha images are transported in processions on decorated boats (opposite, above) and elaborate carriages.

The Koh Samui/Ang Thong archipelago in the Gulf of Thailand comprises some 80 tropical islands. The 50 limestone islands of Ang Thong (above), which can be visited by boat from Koh Samui, were designated a marine national park in 1980. Covered in pristine forest and edged with white sandy beaches, almost all of Ang Thong's islands are uninhabited.

By contrast, nearby Samui island has in recent years become one of Thailand's leading beach destinations. Luckily, the island is large enough to sustain a tourist boom: its fine palm-fringed beaches (above left) and clear waters, ideal for snorkelling and diving (opposite, below), mostly retain an idyllic appearance and modern infrastructure has largely been restricted to developments in keeping with the natural surroundings, as at the Imperial Boat House Hotel (left).

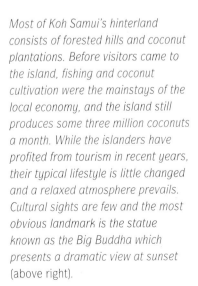

Most of Koh Samui's hinterland consists of forested hills and coconut plantations. Before visitors came to the island, fishing and coconut cultivation were the mainstays of the local economy, and the island still produces some three million coconuts a month. While the islanders have profited from tourism in recent years, their typical lifestyle is little changed and a relaxed atmosphere prevails. Cultural sights are few and the most obvious landmark is the statue known as the Big Buddha which presents a dramatic view at sunset (above right).

Apart from the little town of Na Thon, a ferry port and general service centre for the island, Koh Samui's main focus of interest lies in its superb beaches. Numerous sandy shores and small coves are dotted around the coast, but the best and most popular beaches are on the eastern side of the island. Although its long white sandy strand still presents an idyllic picture, Lamai Beach (left) is the most developed, with bars, restaurants and nightspots hidden behind its fringe of palms.

Koh Samui's northern coast is generally quieter and less developed than the eastern shore and because of this it has gained favour with budget travellers. Mae Nam Beach (above), with a sweeping bay and panoramic sea views out towards the neighbouring island of Koh Pha Ngan, is especially popular.

Directly north of Lamai, Chaweng is perhaps the most beautiful of all Samui's beaches. Stretching for several kilometres, it is also the longest, which allows for picturesque scenes (right) to co-exist with its many resorts, most of which are more upmarket than those of Lamai.

The towns of the southern Gulf coast have character, and an ambience that is typically their own, rather than obvious historical or monumental attractions. The region has a long past dating back to the early centuries AD when the peninsula was a staging-post on the sea route from India to China. The area also achieved prominence during the Srivijaya period (8th to 13th centuries) but little remains to bear witness to what has been a separate and distinguished historical development. The main towns of today serve primarily as fishing ports and commercial centres for their surrounding districts. The cultural heart of the region is Nakhon Si Thammarat, one of the oldest continuously inhabited settlements in the country. The city is known for its fine handicrafts of nielloware and yan lipao basketry and for two ancient dramatic arts, Manhora dance drama and nang thalung shadow puppet theatre (above). Performances often take place at local festivals when Nakhon's streets are filled with processions and parades (left).

Nakhon Si Thammarat is also this region's main religious centre; it is here that Theravada Buddhism was initially introduced from its place of origin in Sri Lanka. Foremost of the city's religious sights is Wat Mahathat, dominated by a massive chedi (right) which enshrines relics of the Buddha, making it the most revered shrine in the South.

A visit to Nakhon offers the best opportunity to see performances of the Manhora dance (below and below right), a classical art form that is unique to the South. With its roots in ancient India and the Indianized dance forms of Java, Manhora is a dance drama that has a strong narrative drive complemented by songs and enlivened by colourful costumes. Modern-day performances, seen at temple fairs and other festive events, are reduced versions of the old full-scale productions, yet the drama manages to retain its essential vitality.

157

Further down the Gulf coast, and almost matching Nakhon Si Thammarat in historical significance, is the old port of Songkhla. Today, nearby Hat Yai, the South's largest city, overshadows this now sleepy little town which, despite its role as the provincial capital, shows little inclination to relinquish its old-world charm in favour of modern commercialism. Attractively sited on a promontory between the sea and the southern end of Thale Sap lagoon, Songkhla combines the attraction of some fine old buildings, including one or two interesting temples with their attendant festive parades (above left), and the easy-going atmosphere of a traditional fishing port where the day's catch is laid out to dry in the sun (left).

Thale Sap is one of several linked lagoons which stretch from Songkhla (above) into neighbouring Phattalung province, comprising Thailand's largest inland body of water. A productive fishing ground, especially for black tiger prawns, Thale Sap also provides a habitat for thousands of mostly migratory birds which are protected in two waterfowl parks, Khu Khut in Songkhla and Thale Noi in Phattalung. Both are intriguing environments where the distinction between land and water is blurred in a strange blend of islands, marshes and open lake.

Below Thale Sap, the bustling, modern city of Hat Yai devotes itself to business and night-time entertainment. Yet even here flower garland markets (right) and other traditional sights are not completely absent.

159

The people of Thailand's southernmost provinces share a cultural heritage with their Malaysian neighbours. Many are Muslim (left) and the Wadin Husen mosque at Narathiwat (top) is one of several important mosques that add their distinctive architecture to the more familiar scenes of Buddhist temples. Among other sights special to the area are caged song birds (above), for which singing contests are held, and the intricately decorated kawlae fishing boats (opposite, above). Fleets of larger fishing boats (opposite, below) attest to the main industry of these far south coastal provinces which, in spite of several fine beaches, have yet to attract the attention of tourism developers.

Across the peninsula on the shores of the Andaman Sea lie Satun and Trang, provinces little visited by travellers, although off the coast of Satun is the Tarutao group of islands, the country's first marine national park. To the north is Krabi province where the fabulous scenery of the twin Phi Phi islands presents the archetypal image of a tropical hideaway, with limestone cliffs, palm groves and white sandy beaches. Shaped like a lopsided butterfly, the larger of the two islands, Phi Phi Don (above), is formed by a narrow strand joining two 'wings' of which the left has high shrub-covered hills and the right a jungle-clad spine flanked on either side by palm-fringed beaches. Most boats to the islands arrive at Tonsai Bay (left), to the right of the isthmus; the village here has expanded to provide more facilities for visitors, especially divers.

Neighbouring Phi Phi Le island has more dramatic scenery than Phi Phi Don and is uninhabited. Though there is only one hotel on Phi Phi Don, many of its bays support beach bungalow resorts so tourism has left its mark on what was once, like its sister island, a site of untouched natural beauty. None the less, pristine beaches are still to be found (above) and the waters surrounding both islands abound in colourful corals and reef life. With spirit shrines (right) adding an exotic touch to what is still superb scenery, Phi Phi remains captivating, and its status as part of the Had Nopparat Marine National Park should afford it protection from excess development.

163

The coastlines of both Krabi (left) and neighbouring Phang-Nga province are among the most scenic in the entire South. Besides picturesque fishing boats (below left) and the stilted villages of fishing communities (below), the coastal scenery is characterized by karst limestone formations thrown up by shifts in the earth's crust some 75 million years ago. On land this has formed sheer cliffs while out at sea the phenomenon appears as hauntingly sculpted islands and rocky outcrops.

The most startling example of this region's seascape is Phang-Nga Bay, where hundreds of karst outcrops dot the water. Fantastically shaped by erosion over the millennia and swathed in tangles of creepers and shrubs, some of the outcrops rise sheer, others are humped or jagged. Some are little more than rocks, while others have precipitous cliffs large enough to conceal caves and grottoes. Most famous of all is the so-called James Bond island (opposite) which was featured in the 1970s film The Man with the Golden Gun.

With clear waters, extensive coral reefs and excellent facilities, the west coast of Thailand's southern peninsula offers the best snorkelling and scuba diving in the country. The warm tropical waters of the Andaman Sea hold a wealth of different types of site, making the area ideal for divers of all levels of proficiency. A string of marine national parks the length of this coast – from the Surin Islands down to Krabi and Koh Lanta, and beyond to Tarutao – now aims to protect the underwater environment from damaging practices of the past and marine life is generally rich and varied. Thailand's all-purpose longtail boats (top) take divers on day trips while fully equipped, live-aboard dive boats cater for longer excursions to remoter destinations such as the Similan Islands (opposite) and the Richelieu Rock.

Coral reefs abound along the coast, especially around the numerous offshore islands. Here, snorkellers as well as divers can revel in the wonders of the underwater world as dazzling reef fish, such as angelfish (above left) and trumpetfish (left), dart among multi-coloured corals, sea fans, sponges and featherstars and around other exotic reef inhabitants, including anemones, starfish, sea cucumbers and Giant Clams.

Phuket, an entire province appended to Phang-Nga by a narrow causeway, is Thailand's largest island and its premier beach resort. The island has an interior of forested hills interrupted by rubber, coconut and pineapple plantations, while strung all along the western coast is a series of beautiful bays with fine sandy beaches (opposite, above). From being a backpacker's paradise in the 1970s, Phuket has rocketed to international tourism stardom and now hosts close to two million visitors annually.

Deluxe resort hotels (opposite, below right) have been built at all the main beaches, but Phuket's size prevents a sense of overcrowding and one can still always find an idyllic spot all to oneself (right). Beach sellers (below) and typical longtail boats (opposite, below left) maintain a traditional air in spite of extensive modern development and Phuket has generally been successful in maintaining a balance between providing facilities for visitors and preserving natural beauty.

The beach is not Phuket's only attraction and the island has a history and culture quite independent of its present fame as a holiday resort. Known long ago to Arab and Indian seafarers, and later Western explorers and traders, Phuket became one of Thailand's wealthiest provinces when tin mining boomed in the 19th century. After the tin was mined out, the cultivation of rubber trees (opposite, above right) was developed and remains a major source of income. More recently cultured pearl farming (opposite, above left) has become part of the economy. This diversity of activity is paralleled in the island's cultural make-up. Over the centuries Phuket has been a melting pot and is today characterized by an intriguing blend of Thai, Chinese and Muslim traditions, with distinctions most easily seen in the juxtaposition of Thai Buddhist temples (above), mosques and Chinese shrines. The Vegetarian Festival (opposite, below), during which devotees perform acts of self-mortification, is one long-standing tradition established by the early Chinese immigrants.

Much of the island's hilly green interior is now devoted to plantations but primary rainforest can still be seen in Khao Phra Tieo National Park. Back on the coast, the unique geological formations and mangrove eco-systems of Phuket's offshore islands – a reminder of the area's prehistoric past – can today be explored by kayak (right).

171

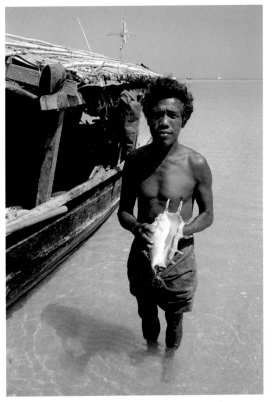

To the north of Phuket lie the Marine National Parks of the beautiful Similan Islands and, beyond, the equally idyllic Surin Islands. Pristine, white-sand coves, crystal-clear turquoise waters, and a profusion of exotic marine life draw visitors to their unspoilt shores. Both areas offer top-class diving and snorkelling and the Similans (left and above), in particular, have a breathtaking variety of exciting sites to dive.

Little developed, and with few facilities, both groups of islands are largely uninhabited except for Park officials and, on Koh Surin Tai, a community of traditional island people known as 'sea gypsies' (top).

INDEX

PHOTOGRAPHIC ACKNOWLEDGEMENTS

The publishers extend their thanks to the following people who kindly loaned their photographs for inclusion in this book. With the exception of those listed below, the photographs in the book were taken by **Gerald Cubitt**.

Artasia Press (John Everingham): 13 (left), 70 (above), 97 (above), 129 (above), 133, 155 (above)

Asia Images (Matthew Burns): 153 (below right), 155 (below); **(Allen W. Hopkins):** 127 (below), 136 (below)

Axiom (Jim Holmes): 88 (above)

Crescent Press Agency (David Henley): 156 (above)

Ron Emmons: 14 (below), 52 (above), 54 (above and below left), 55, 62 (above left), 63 (above right)

Footprints (Nick Hanna): 139 (below), 150 (above right); **(Haydn Jones):** 57 (above)

Michael Freeman: 94 (above right), 97 (below left and below right), 103 (below right), 164 (centre)

Jill Gocher: 1, 2, 3, 28 (left), 43 (above left), 109 (below right), 157 (below left and below right), 158 (above left and below), 161 (above), 163 (below), 164 (top)

Mark Graham: 152 (above right)

David Holdsworth: 65 (above right and below), 107 (top)

The Hutchison Library (Michael MacIntyre): 10

Christina Jansen: 153 (above right)

Maurice Joseph: 5, 99 (below left)

Norma Joseph: 41 (centre left)

Khun Akorn Restaurant: 37, 109 (above)

Neil McAllister: 99 (below right), 151 (below)

Keith Mundy: 22, 25 (above), 34 (right), 35 (above right), 74, 81 (below right), 82 (below left and below right), 88 (below), 89 (above left and above right), 96 (above), 103 (below left), 120 (top left, centre and below), 123 (below left), 128 (above left and below left), 129 (below), 173 (above right)

New Holland (Publishers) Ltd: 123 (below right)

Oceanic Impressions (Mark Strickland): 19 (above right), 138 (top, middle and below left), 162 (above), 166 (all three subjects), 167, 168 (below left), 171 (above and below), 172, 173 (below right)

The Oriental Hotel, Bangkok: 25 (below)

PhotoBank (Adrian Baker): 106, 135 (above); **(Jeanetta Baker):** 42 (left); **(Peter Baker):** 11, 32, 39, 83 (above), 110 (above), 113 (above right), 123 (above), 134 (above), 144 (below right), 146 (below), 165, 170 (above right)

PictureBank Photo Library: 53 (above), 99 (above), 113 (below), 122 (above), 143, 169 (above and below)

Tourism Authority of Thailand: 20, 31, 35 (above left), 41 (above right and below left), 96 (below), 109 (below left), 122 (below left), 131 (below left), 151 (above), 157 (above right), 170 (below)

Travel Ink (Abbie Enock): 29, 65 (above left), 66 (above); **(Allan Hartley):** 75, 91 (above)

Zefa Pictures: 154 (left)